SPEND THE DAY HAPPILY, PUT PERFUMES AND FINE OILS TO THY

NOSE, GARLANDS AND LOTUS FLOWERS ON THE BODY OF YOUR

LOVE WHO SITS BESIDE YOU, CAST ALL EVIL BEHIND YOU AND

THINK ONLY OF JOY, UNTIL THAT DAY COMES WHEN YOU

REACH THE PORT IN THE LAND THAT LOVES SILENCE...

(NEW KINGDOM BANQUET SONG)

OILS AND PERFUMES OF ANCIENT EGYPT

BY JOANN FLETCHER

BRITISH MUSEUM 🏛 PRESS

IMPORTANT NOTICE

The information given in the text is based on ancient sources
and is not intended to be used as a medical guide in any way.
No liability will be accepted by either the publishers
or the author following any accident or injury arising from
the use or misuse of any of the materials referred to.

© 1998 The Trustees of the British Museum

First published in 1998 by British Museum Press
A division of The British Museum Company Ltd
46 Bloomsbury Street, London WC1B 3QQ

ISBN 0 7141 2703 5

Designed by Harry Green

Printed in Great Britain
by Butler & Tanner Ltd, Frome, Somerset

FRONT COVER: Detail of a wall painting from the tomb
of Nebamun. Thebes. New Kingdom. (British Museum)

FRONTISPIECE: King Rameses II anoints the cult statue of Osiris.
Painted temple relief at Abydos. New Kingdom.

CONTENTS

ACKNOWLEDGEMENTS

I would like to thank the following individuals and organizations for their help and assistance:

David Beaumont; Sian Edwards-Davies; Janice Eyres; Prof. Mahmoud Ezzamel; Alan & Christine Fildes; Joyce Filer; Garry and Susan Fletcher; Katherine Fletcher; DrDiane France; Christopher Hedley (MNIMH); Shirley Lancaster; Jackie Ligo; Sarah Lucas; Sharon McDermott (MBSY); Gail McKinnon; Joan McMahon; Christine Marshall; Anne Murray; Dr Paul Nicholson; Dr. Margaret Serpico; Ali Hassan Sheba and family; Carole Walker; Roxie Walker; Jeanne Whitehurst; the BioAnthropology Foundation; the NILE Organisation; and members of the Hierakonpolis Expedition Team, so many of whom so willingly took part in my experiments with ancient Egyptian aromatherapy, reflexology and massage.

INTRODUCTION

In recent years there has been a phenomenal growth in the use of 'alternative' medicines and therapies, although a number of so-called 'New Age' practices are actually very ancient indeed. This is particularly true of massage, reflexology and aromatherapy, forms of which were practised in ancient Egypt, using oils and perfumes. The Egyptians were the first to use many of the oils and perfumes we are familiar with today. Their practical, therapeutic, social and religious uses were depicted on tomb and temple walls and recorded in literary texts, many of which were later copied by Greek and Roman scholars who looked to Egypt as the source of all wisdom. It is from such documentation that we are able to reconstruct so many of the original recipes and remedies. We are also fortunate that Egypt's dry environment has preserved so much evidence of the ancient Egyptians' daily lives and burial customs, providing archaeological remains to support the artistic and literary evidence.

Of all the oils the Egyptians used almond oil was regarded as one of the finest; it formed the base of some of their most famous perfumes and medicines and was also valued for massage. The evocative essences of lotus, cedar and cinnamon were also widely prized, for their own scent as well as their value in a whole range of fragrant recipes and remedies for use in social and domestic contexts, religious ritual, medicine, massage and mummification. These three important fragrances neatly represent the ancient Egyptian notions of life and death: the beautiful lotus flower symbolized creation and new life, whilst the cedar and cinnamon used in the mummification process represented death and the afterlife. Lotus, cedar and cinnamon also played a central role in religious ritual, which involved lavish offerings of costly perfumes, huge floral bouquets and thick clouds of sweet incense, the power of fragrance being one of the ways the Egyptians bridged the gap between the mortal and divine worlds. The same idea can also be found in funerary rituals, which were designed to revive the dead by reawakening their senses, the sense of smell restored with the perfumes used in daily life and regarded as so essential in the afterlife.

HISTORY

Oils and perfumes were used in Egypt even before it was unified into a single state around 3100 BC. Although burials from this pre-literate 'Predynastic' period are generally little more than hollows in the sand, the presence of grave goods indicates that the early Egyptians already believed in an afterlife. In addition to such essentials as food and drink, the dead were often buried with a range of cosmetics and the raw materials for their preparation. Perfumes made of resin, lime and oil have been discovered in Predynastic graves, along with ingredients such as juniper and henna, oil-producing seeds and imported coniferous resins. One royal tomb at Abydos (c.3000 BC) contained jars complete with their original contents of coniferous resin mixed with plant oils and animal fats, and the excavators of another royal tomb at the site found the sandy floors saturated with perfumes to a depth of 1 metre (3 feet); the scent was so strong that it still pervaded the whole tomb.

This lavish use of perfumes in burials continued into the Old Kingdom, and numerous tomb scenes from this

period show the tomb owners inhaling perfumes and flowers whose scent was thought sufficiently potent to restore their senses. The earliest evidence for massage also dates from this time: contemporary reliefs in tombs at Saqqara show both foot massage and reflexology, whilst scenes from the temple of Niuserre show the king's feet being massaged with oil. Tomb walls also portray scenes of perfume production and jars marked with the perfumes they contain, known as the 'Seven Sacred Oils': Festival Perfume, *Hekenu* (Praise) Oil, *Sefeti* Oil, *Nekhenem* Oil,

Tewat Oil, Best Cedar Oil and Best Libyan Oil. Listed in the Pyramid Texts, the oldest body of religious writings in the world, these oils appear on tomb walls, offering slabs, coffins and papyri. They were used in daily temple ritual, funerary rites, cosmetics and medicines, and although only the wealthy were likely to own a full set of oils, most people could afford at least one or two.

The Egyptians often travelled far afield to obtain the materials to make their oils and perfumes, and by the Middle Kingdom the myrrh imported from 'Punt' – the region around Somalia – was added to the seven existing Sacred Oils. Perfume jars of this date from Dahshur still contain myrrh and pistacia resin, and a jar found in a tomb at el-Bersheh contained cedar resin that had been used to preserve the internal organs of the mummy. The use of such fragrant imports in mummification is referred to in literature of the time, one text bemoaning the state of the nation when supplies of the cedar and oils used in mummification had run dry. In the famous Middle Kingdom story of Sinuhe, the once-exiled courtier returns to a hero's welcome in Egypt. After being anointed with the best oil (instead of the inferior grease he had used when abroad) he is given a palace with 'choice perfumes in every room'. Many of the raw materials for such perfumes,

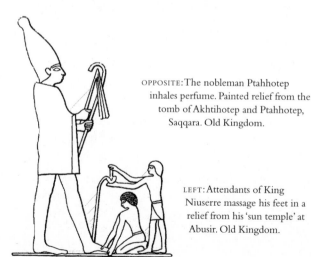

OPPOSITE: The nobleman Ptahhotep inhales perfume. Painted relief from the tomb of Akhtihotep and Ptahhotep, Saqqara. Old Kingdom.

LEFT: Attendants of King Niuserre massage his feet in a relief from his 'sun temple' at Abusir. Old Kingdom.

including myrrh, ladanum, pistacia resin, cinnamon, perfumed oil and frankincense, were imported from Punt, where they were imagined to be guarded by a huge golden serpent, the 'Lord of Punt'. So fabled was this land of perfume that even its birds were said to be anointed with myrrh and have claws full of unguent.

Four hundred years later, scenes in the temple of the female pharaoh Hatshepsut at Deir el-Bahari record a great trading expedition to the land of Punt to obtain the fragrant woods and resins used in temple rituals. The mission also took incense tree saplings back to Egypt: 'thirty-one fresh *antiuw* (resin) trees brought back as wonders of Punt' are shown on the temple walls. Several of Hatshepsut's New Kingdom successors also attempted to import trees and plants. During his military campaigns to Syria and Asia Minor the great conqueror Tuthmosis III also found time to collect rare plants, which he sent back to Egypt to be planted in the gardens of Karnak temple; the relief scenes recording these exotic plants are regarded as 'the oldest herbal in the world'. Such temple gardens supplied the millions of flowers, herbs and spices used in rituals, medicines and perfume production; at Amarna, traces of almonds were found along with imported jars of resin and quantities of incense at the city's temple sites.

Botanical Gardens of Tuthmosis III. Relief from Karnak temple. New Kingdom.

The funerary uses of oils and perfumes also continued into the New Kingdom. The burial of the young pharaoh Tutankhamun in the Valley of the Kings at Thebes was accompanied by huge quantities of perfumes, oils, incense, flowers and herbs – his mummy was doused in sacred perfumes, swathed in floral garlands and surrounded by jars originally containing over 350 litres (77 gallons) of perfume! On the back of the golden throne found in the tomb is a massage scene involving the king and his wife Ankhesenamun.

Many perfume ingredients were still imported. At

Amarna, bulk imports of scented resins were found inside Canaanite amphorae, and a number of other oils and perfumes were imported from Cyprus, Asia Minor, Babylon and the Kadesh region. Scenes on the walls of the hypostyle hall of Seti I at Karnak temple depict conquered Asiatics extracting cedar resin for export to Egypt, and Seti himself announced how he had conquered southern lands in order to bring the gods 'tribute of gum and myrrh and cinnamon and all the pleasant sweet wood of Punt'. Before setting out on campaign the army itself was anointed with imported perfumes, while a contemporary text also refers to 'the young men of the city in festive attire every day with sweet oil upon their heads'. Even workmen received regular supplies of ointment 'for anointing their heads every week': the first recorded strike in history occurred

Queen Ankhesenamun massages her husband King Tutankhamun with perfumed oil. On the back of the king's golden throne, tomb of Tutankhamun, Valley of the Kings, Thebes. New Kingdom. (Cairo Museum)

during the reign of Rameses III (1165 BC) when supplies of oil to the tomb builders in the Valley of the Kings were interrupted. The same king was rather more generous in his donations to the temples, however, importing incense trees and vast quantities of cinnamon, offering floral bouquets by the million and planting olive groves to supply the temples with lamp oil.

The use of oils and perfumes continued down the centuries and perfume jars containing resins and oils have been found in tombs of the Late Period. The Greek poet Homer stated that Egypt was a fertile land 'rich in herbs'; his fellow countryman Herodotus, visiting Egypt in c.450 BC, also commented on the use of perfumes and spices when he wrote that the myrrh and cinnamon used in mummification at that time were obtained from Arabia, where it was apparently guarded by mythical creatures. A century or so later another Greek writer, Theophrastus, stated in his work *Concerning Odours* that Egyptian perfumes were undoubtedly the best in the world, relating that one Greek perfume merchant 'had Egyptian perfume in his shop for eight years…and it was still in good condition, in fact better than fresh perfume!'

In the fourth century BC, the Greek Ptolemaic dynasty established their new capital at Alexandria on the Mediterranean coast. By this time many perfume ingredients, including frankincense, myrrh, cinnamon, galbanum and cardamom were being imported from as far away as India, and Alexandria soon became the greatest trading centre of the ancient world. The Ptolemies also continued pharaonic traditions in their lavish use of perfumes. The great temples they built to honour their adopted gods at Edfu and Dendera included perfume laboratories where the ritual perfumes and ever-increasing varieties of incense were

King Rameses III offers perfume to the gods. Relief from his funerary temple, Medinet Habu. New Kingdom.

produced, and in the perfume factories of Alexandria materials imported from Palestine, Syria, Yemen, Asia Minor and India were combined with native products to produce oils and perfumes which were then exported, mainly to Rome.

Cleopatra VII, the last of the Ptolemies, was reputed to have used a different perfume for every part of her body – her perfumed hand cream alone was said to cost the exorbitant sum of 400 denarii. However, since she owned the huge and valuable estates which produced the perfumes in the first place she could easily afford such luxuries and obviously used them to great effect: Shakespeare, writing 1600 years later, recalls how the perfumed breeze announced the arrival of her cedarwood ship with its lily-scented sails. So adept was Cleopatra in the dramatic use of perfumes that she was credited with writing a 'Book of Beautification' in 50 BC and was regularly quoted by Roman authors as late as the seventh century AD.

Cleopatra VII offers to the gods. Relief on rear wall of temple of Hathor, Dendera. Graeco-Roman Period.

In fact, Rome was the main market for the highly lucrative Egyptian perfume industry, even with the taxes and duty levied on imports of frankincense. Perfume dealers had to pay taxes of 60 drachmae a month or the equivalent in spices, but so lucrative was the trade that perfume merchants were still rumoured to make a hundredfold profit. In his book *Natural History*, the Roman Pliny the Elder echoed the comments of earlier Greek writers when he stated that Egypt was the country best suited to perfume production, while his contemporary Dioscorides gave detailed recipes for perfumes in his *Herbal*. Roman poets such as Ovid also wrote on the subject of perfumes, and the female poet Lais composed a risqué work designed for 'a special class of woman'! Although unaware of the religious and mystical overtones of many of the Pharaonic fragrances, Lais did at least understand the Egyptians' appreciation for the sensual uses of perfumes, and it was only with the sanctimonious attitude to the body demonstrated by the early Christians that the Egyptian art of perfumery was finally lost. 'Pagan' habits of indulgence and luxury were forbidden and abstinence was made a virtue: the faint wisp of incense permitted in church was soon the only memory of the billowing clouds once offered daily at every shrine in Egypt.

INGREDIENTS

The ancient Egyptians used a huge range of native and imported materials to produce their fragrant oils and perfumes. However, it can prove difficult to identify specific ingredients from the names given in the ancient texts, and there are still a number of plants whose ancient names we do not know. Where the ancient name is known, it has been given in brackets.

∿ OILS ∿

Choice of oils depended on wealth and status: the finest oils could only be afforded by the wealthy, and castor oil – at half the price of sesame oil – was the cheapest and the most widely used. Almond, moringa, balanos, safflower, olive and linseed oils were all produced, as were radish, tiger nut, lettuce, poppy and colocynth oils to a lesser extent.

ALMOND OIL is extracted from the kernels of the almond tree (*awenet*). Almonds were found at the New Kingdom workmen's village at Amarna and in Tutankhamun's tomb, but the pale yellow or colourless oil was generally imported from Greece. Almond oil was used in the production of Metopion perfume and fragrant unguents, for therapeutic massage and in the treatment of bad skin and facial spots.

BALANOS OIL is derived from the kernels of a small native tree which grows wild, and was used from Predynastic times onwards. It is pale yellow, odourless and tasteless, and whilst not suitable to be taken internally it was extensively used in cosmetic preparations, being reputed to clear the complexion of spots and blemishes. As the most viscous of the oils it was also the one most suitable for perfume production: the Megaleion and Mendesian perfumes had a base of balanos oil mixed with varying blends of myrrh, cinnamon and resin.

CASTOR OIL is obtained from the seeds of the native castor oil plant (*degem*). Castor oil seeds, which are highly toxic and need careful handling, have been found in Predynastic burials at el-Badari and Maadi. The strongly scented, inedible oil is slow to go rancid, and was used both as a lamp oil and for anointing and massaging the body. The Ebers Medical Papyrus has a whole section entitled 'Knowledge of what can be made from the castor oil plant, as found in the ancient writings and useful to people'. Castor oil was reputed to cure stomach illnesses and constipation, skin diseases, illness in the limbs and diseases caused by demons; it was also used as a headlice lotion and hair restorer.

COLOCYNTH OIL, a golden yellow oil said to cure mange, is derived from the seeds of a native ground plant (*djaret*) found at several Neolithic and Predynastic sites.

LETTUCE OIL from the seeds of the native edible plant (*aft*) is reputed to promote male fertility (it is interesting that lettuce was sacred to Min, the god of fertility, and was forbidden to certain priests!). The oil was used as a hair-restorer and also to treat stomach pain, earache and eye complaints.

LINSEED OIL comes from the seeds of the native flax plant (*mehy*), which has been found at Predynastic sites and

is shown being harvested in funerary scenes. The yellow oil, though prone to rancidity, was used externally in pain relief preparations and blended with sycamore figs, honey and ochre to treat the finger and toe nails.

MORINGA OIL (*bak*) comes from the kernels of the small native moringa tree. The sweet-tasting, pale yellow and odourless oil is slow to go rancid and was used extensively in cosmetic, medical and massage preparations. During the New Kingdom (*c.*1300 BC) it became fashionable among male city-dwellers as a sweet-smelling hair oil that conveniently doubled as a headlice lotion, while applied neat to the skin it prevented mosquito bites. It was frequently mixed with honey in medical remedies to treat head and stomach aches, and was also used in massage blends recommended as 'soothing' when mixed with frankincense, myrrh and cinnamon, 'refreshing' when combined with frankincense, cyperus grass, salt and fat, and 'anti-inflammatory' when added to alkanet, powdered carob and resin.

OLIVE OIL, extracted from the fruit of a small slow-growing tree (*jedtuw*), was largely imported from Syria and Greece, although olive stones dating from the Middle

Kingdom have been found at Memphis. The tree itself was a late introduction to Egypt, grown in the Fayum and Memphis, around Thebes and at Heliopolis, where Rameses III planted an olive grove to supply oil for lighting the temple of the sun god Ra. Olive oil was also valuable for steeping aromatic myrtle leaves and henna seeds. Sampsuchinon perfume was made from marjoram, thyme, cassia, southernwood, nasturtium and myrtle covered in olive oil. The distinctive smell of the oil could be removed with wine, although the Greeks preferred the smell of their own olive oil to that of the Egyptians. The Roman writer Dioscorides considered it good for massage, 'keeping out chills and preparing the body for action'. Olive oil was also used for ritual divination.

POPPY OIL extracted from the edible seeds of the native flower (*shepen*) is yellow with a pleasant smell and taste when cold pressed, although heat extraction gives a darker oil with an unpleasant smell. The seeds, found as early as the Old Kingdom, were used in a massage unguent of carob pulp and boiled hippopotamus skin. The sedative use of poppy oil, which relied on its opium content, seems confirmed by the reported discovery of morphine in a jar of New Kingdom date.

RADISH OIL comes from the seeds of a native plant (*semuw*). Found at Middle Kingdom sites, it was one of the most common oil crops in Roman Egypt, used for cooking and anointing and occasionally to treat skin diseases.

SAFFLOWER OIL is derived from the seeds of a plant (*katcha*) which was introduced from Western Asia as early as the Middle Kingdom. The bland, pale yellow oil has a slightly unpleasant odour and was used against insect and scorpion bites.

SESAME OIL (*nekhekh*) comes from the tiny seeds of a native plant (*ikuw*) which have been found in Predynastic graves and Tutankhamun's tomb. The pale-coloured oil was used in the preparation of perfume and unguents for massage. During the New Kingdom, the tomb-builders working in the Valley of the Kings were supplied with sesame oil for culinary use and as lamp oil.

TIGER NUT OIL was extracted from the edible tubers or 'tiger nuts' (*shenyta*) of the native cyperus plant. In use since Predynastic times, tiger nut oil is similar to olive oil in that it is slow to go rancid; it was also used in perfume production.

∾ FATS ∾

Although animal-based perfumes such as musk and ambergris were unknown in ancient Egypt, animal fats were employed in perfume. The fats used for such purposes are generally named in the ancient texts as *segnen* or *adj* and were generally a by-product of domestic and ritual butchery, derived from cattle, sheep, goats, donkeys and waterfowl; the fat of specifically sacrificial animals was referred to as *ken*. Goose fat was made for a religious festival at Amarna and the tomb of a Late Period Theban official contained a jar of beef fat mixed with cedar oil.

Ancient medical texts also recommend the fat of the hippopotamus, ostrich, ibex, lion, cat, crocodile, snake, hedgehog and mouse, perhaps in the hope that the animal's characteristics would be present in their fat. This may explain why cat grease was used to get rid of rodents in the house, hedgehog fat was used in a baldness cure, and snake fat was used in a massage unguent to enhance suppleness. Rather less clear is why ibex fat should have been used in a headache remedy, hippopotamus fat in a dandruff treatment and a combination of lion, hippo, crocodile and snake fat in a hair restorer.

∾ FLOWERS ∾

CHAMOMILE is a native plant with yellow flowers. According to the Greeks, the Egyptians dedicated chamomile to the sun god because it cured hot fevers. The flowers were present in the garlands on Tutankhamun's mummy and traces of the plant were found on the body of Rameses II, possibly due to its use as an insecticide. Chamomile oil is known to combat bacteria, and its flowers also produce a strong dye.

LILY is a cream-coloured native flower with a delicious sweet, heavy scent. Late Period tomb scenes show women gathering lily flowers and making Susinon perfume. The soothing aromatic oil made from the flowers was used in medicine to treat 'female complaints'. It was

Hedgehog pot. Middle Kingdom. (British Museum)

associated with female spirituality and sensuality, and it was the fragrance that scented the sails of Cleopatra VII's royal barge.

LOTUS (*seshen*) is the name commonly given to the native aquatic waterlily, a common motif throughout the Pharaonic period and the heraldic symbol of southern Egypt. Both the white lotus and the sweet-smelling blue lotus were favourite garden plants, and their flowers were used indoors for decorative garlands and bouquets. The lotus was associated with the idea of creation and rebirth, being described as 'the flower which came into being at the beginning'. Emerging from the dark waters of primordial chaos to open its petals at dawn, it symbolized the morning sun emerging from the darkness of night, and so had strong solar connections. The flower was sacred to the young god Nefertem and was one of the commonest offerings in temples – Rameses III presented over 3,000 lotus bouquets to the god Amun alone. It was also an important part of funerary ritual, in which the mummy of

Nefertem, young god of the lotus flower. Tomb of King Horemheb, Valley of the Kings. New Kingdom.

the deceased was adorned with garlands of lotus flowers, and in numerous tomb scenes the scent of the flower is inhaled to restore the senses of the deceased. Its luscious perfume was said to create a happy disposition: lotus oil was considered an aphrodisiac, and was a favourite fragrance for Egyptian priestesses. The lotus was used in medical preparations to treat liver disease and the oil to reduce temperatures. A fragrant therapeutic unguent for the head blended lotus flowers and myrrh (although the leaves steeped in oil and placed on the head of a 'hated woman' made her hair fall out!).

POPPY (*shepen*) was a common garden plant whose beautiful scarlet flowers contained both oil-producing seeds and opium. Poppies were also used decoratively in floral garlands and in bouquets for domestic, ritual and funerary purposes.

SAFFLOWER (*katcha*) is an annual plant with yellow-orange flowers and oil-producing seeds which were also used as a source of dye. It was introduced from Western Asia some time during the Middle Kingdom.

SWEET FLAG (*keni*) is a common perennial garden plant whose aromatic root was considered an aphrodisiac. Sweet flag was used extensively in perfume production to fix the fragrance and to sweeten the base oils and fats. It also had a medicinal use as a treatment for stomach ailments.

⋙ HERBS ⋙

BRYONY (*khasyt*) is a perennial native herb. Burnt as an incense to cure demonic possession, it was also used medically in an unguent for headaches, and added to a fig and raisin drink to ease stomach aches as well as other internal disorders.

CORIANDER (*shaw*) is a native herb with a rather sweet, spicy scent thought by the Egyptians to be an aphrodisiac. The best coriander was said to grow in Egypt. It was one of the offerings given to the gods by the king, and its seeds were discovered in Tutankhamun's tomb. In perfume production it was used to neutralize the smell of certain oils and fat. In medicine it was mixed with honey to heal sores, herpes and broken bones and was given in a drink to ease

stomach aches; it was also a snake-bite antidote and was added to baths to expel fever.

FENUGREEK (*hemayet*) is an annual native herb whose nutritious seeds, found as early as 3000 BC, were used in a famous rejuvenating recipe and in a number of medical remedies; it is still used in Egypt for treating stomach upsets.

MARJORAM (*semsobek*) is a common native herb with small pink or white flowers. Its warm, slightly spicy scent was thought to confer longevity and it was used in mummy garlands. Sacred to the crocodile god Sobek, marjoram was the major ingredient in the sharp-smelling Sampsuchum unguent, while Sampsuchinon oil, made of marjoram and other herbs in olive oil, was 'a warming oil best used with honey'. Marjoram was also used medicinally to ease toothache, earache headache and rheumatism.

MINT (*tis*) is a native perennial herb with a strong penetrating menthol fragrance said to 'rouse the conscious mind'. It was used in some recipes for Kyphi perfume and was given in a warm drink to ward off fever (modern Egyptians still use mint in this way, adding it to hot tea).

Mint also acts as an insect repellent and its leaves were found in a bouquet from a Late Period tomb.

THYME (*tchaa-iti*) is a native herb whose pungent scent was thought in ancient times to encourage bravery. It was used in perfume production (*thymos* is the Greek word for 'smell' or 'perfume'), in cooking, in headache remedies and as a fumigatory repellent to ward off 'venomous creatures'; a single sprig of thyme was discovered in Tutankhamun's tomb.

ᴡ SPICES ᴡ

ANISEED (*inset*) is a native umbelliferous plant whose oil-producing fruit and brown-grey seeds are strongly aromatic, reminiscent of liquorice. The seeds were used for culinary purposes and medically as an internal stomach remedy and for toothache; the warming oil was also used for massage.

CARDAMOM was an imported sweet spice. Its dark brown seeds were used to scent and thicken aromatic unguents, particularly Metopion perfume, which smelt predominantly of cardamom and myrrh. It was also considered effective against rheumatism and joint stiffness.

CUMIN (*tepnen*) is a native annual herb with spicy seeds. Cumin seeds were offered to the sun god by the king and were found in a pot in the tomb of Tutankhamun. They were used in cooking and had numerous medicinal uses: in a fragrant headache unguent with myrrh and lotus flowers, in an ointment for the skin, in digestive remedies and in a fruit drink for asthma. Cumin was also used by women as an aid to conception.

ᴡ SHRUBS ᴡ

ALKANET (*nesti*) is a native plant whose roots were used to treat inflammation and were a source of red dye for many perfumes and temple candles.

CYPERUS (*giw*) is a native sedge plant whose leaves were widely employed in perfume manufacture as a thickening agent and to neutralize the odours of certain fats and oils. It was also an ingredient in various preparations, including Kyphi perfume, a 'refreshing' frankincense ointment and a wrinkle treatment.

HENNA (*henuw*) is a native shrub whose leaves, seeds and cream or pink flowers were used as early as the Predynastic period. The best quality henna was said to come from

Canopus in the Delta. Its seeds and sweetly fragrant flowers were used in perfume: the seeds, boiled in olive oil, were crushed and strained to produce Cyprinum perfume: the leaves, mixed with flax and steeped in oil, were recommended as a hair restorer. From Predynastic times a paste made of powdered henna leaves was used to stain the hair, skin and nails red; the earliest evidence of this technique dates from *c.*3500 BC and the tradition continues in modern Egypt, along with the use of henna in headache and heatstroke remedies.

MYRTLE (*khetdes*) is a native aromatic shrub whose leaves, flowers and fruit have a fresh, slightly sweet fragrance. In perfume production, the leaves were steeped in olive oil which then absorbed the fragrance; it was also an ingredient of Sampsuchinon perfume. Myrtle was also burnt as an incense for ritual and medical purposes. It was blended with frankincense to treat stiff limbs, mixed with honey for pain relief, added to beer in a cough remedy, and used in an oily hair preparation.

WORMWOOD (*sam*) is a perennial native shrub with bitter aromatic leaves used in medical remedies including drinks to cure coughs and inflammations. It was also used

in a soothing massage unguent and its stimulant qualities were said to ease fatigue in travellers, Pliny noting it was good for circulation.

⌇ WOODS ⌇

ACACIA (*shendet*) is a native tree whose aromatic wood, leaves, white-yellow flowers, pods and gum were mainly used in medicine. The crushed and bruised wood was said to contain magical healing properties, while the leaves were drunk in a cough mixture and applied to wounds, fractures and swollen limbs for their therapeutic astringent effect; the flowers were used for skin problems.

CAROB (*nedjem*) pods from the native tree were used extensively in cosmetic preparations and as a deodorant body rub. In medicine they feature in remedies for burnt skin, in a sweet unguent to dry up wounds and in many recipes for eye diseases.

CEDAR (*ash*) has a dry woody smell which blends well with cinnamon. The aromatic wood, resin and oil were imported from the Lebanon area as early as the Predynastic period, and jars of coniferous resin mixed with oil have been found in Predynastic graves and in an early royal tomb at Abydos. A small pot of a similar mixture found in Tutankhamun's tomb was labelled *ash* and a Theban tomb of the Late Period contained a jar of beef tallow mixed with cedar oil. Cedar's resiny fragrance acted as an insect repellent, and medical texts recommended it in a honey face wash, mixed with fermented plant juice as a wrinkle treatment, and as a hair restorer (it is still used in hair tonics because of its therapeutic action on the scalp). It was also used to treat swelling, and as a relaxing and calming massage oil to 'soften the limbs'; its softening properties were enhanced by mixing it with frankincense. Cedar oil was also used extensively in ritual: 'Best Cedar Oil' is one of the Seven Sacred Oils named in the Pyramid Texts. It was used to anoint the statues of the gods during daily temple ritual, and played an important part in funerary rites, where it was used to anoint the mummy and preserve the internal organs. The Roman writer Dioscorides stated that cedar 'is the preservative of the dead, hence some have called it "the life of him who is dead"'.

CINNAMON (*tishepses*) has a spicy, sharp, sweet scent which blends well with cedar. As early as 2000 BC, the aromatic bark and leaves were imported from Punt as part of an extensive trade network maintained by later New King-dom monarchs such as Hatshepsut, Seti I and Rameses III, who offered no less than one whole log, 400 measures and 302 bundles of cinnamon to the gods. Dioscorides described cinnamon as 'profitable for many things', particularly the production of Mendesian, Megaleion and Susinon perfumes, while Pliny recommended a cinnamon-based perfume for men. However, care had to be taken in blending these so the cinnamon did not dominate the other ingredients. Cinnamon was used alone as an aphrodisiac fragrance: the oil was sprinkled over beds and the wood burnt as an incense to scent both the clothes and the surroundings. As one of the strongest antiseptics in nature, cinnamon was also used in medical preparations – in soothing, antiseptic massage unguents, foot oils and a remedy for gum ulcers. Cinnamon oil was also extensively used in the process of mummification, and indeed the scent of cinnamon oil rubbed over the skins of mummies still lingers today.

DATE PALM (*beneret*) is a native tree dating back to the Predynastic period and is an integral part of the Egyptian landscape. Its edible fruit is made into a wine which was frequently used to dilute strong fragrances, to sweeten certain fats and oils and as the base of Kyphi perfume. Date wine was also used in the mummification process and in the preparation of medical unguents; date juice was used in a wax mixture to treat swollen legs and the kernels in an oily hair restorer.

JUNIPER (*wan*) has a clear, resiny, peppery fragrance. The imported berries of the trees were found in Predynastic burials and at the Middle Kingdom town of Kahun, where they had been carefully stored in a small wooden box with a sliding lid. Juniper berries were found in a basket in Tutankhamun's tomb as well as scattered among his mummy wrappings. Juniper oil was also used to anoint the body during the mummification process. Juniper was one of the many ingredients in the ritual perfume Kyphi and both the berries and wood were burnt as incense. Its cosmetic applications included its use as a lip colour and a hair dye, and it features in medical preparations to cure headaches, asthma and indigestion. Juniper oil was employed in therapeutic massage and is known to ease aching joints.

SYCAMORE FIG (*nehet*) is a native tree whose sap, leaves and fruit were extensively used in medical remedies to help toothache, ease the stomach, treat tumours and broken bones. The fruit was used in an unguent to soothe stiff limbs and the sap in a hair-removing cream.

⋙ RESINS ⋙

FRANKINCENSE (*antiuw?*) is a spicy, woody, aromatic gum-resin obtained by cutting into the wood of trees of the Boswellia family. The resin is collected in large, tear-shaped yellow globules, the paler in colour the better in quality – the premium resin is referred to as 'white incense' in the ancient texts. Frankincense was imported from southern Arabia and also from the land of Punt (Somalia). Scenes at Hatshepsut's temple at Deir el-Bahari show the import of both the raw material and the trees, whose cultivation was also attempted by several of her royal successors, Tuthmosis III, Amenhotep II and Rameses III. Frankincense trees were planted in the temple gardens of Memphis and Thebes by Rameses III to provide a constant supply of resin for ritual purposes. Frankincense was used extensively for funerary purposes and in perfume production, in cosmetic preparations for wrinkles and for sweetening the breath. It was an important ingredient in a scented 'soothing unguent' to massage stiff limbs, and was also used to dry up wounds, treat burns and scars and tackle asthma, headaches and stomach aches.

GALBANUM is an imported green gum resin obtained from incisions in the stem of the umbelliferous plant Sulphur Wort. Then as now, it was used as a fixative in perfume production: Metopion perfume was named after the Egyptian name for the Sulphur Wort plant, though given its rather unpleasant musky scent, it was important that the galbanum did not dominate the blend. Galbanum was mainly used as an insect repellent in medicine, as a treatment for aching feet and combined with beeswax in the mummification process.

LADANUM (*iber*) was a dark brown-black resin obtained from the leaves of the Cistus tree and imported from the Levant. It was made into small cakes to be used as incense and is also found in headache remedies.

MYRRH (*antiuw?*) is a smoky, musky, bitter aromatic gum-resin obtained from cutting into the green bark of trees of the Commiphora family. The dark yellow-red aromatic gum resin was imported from Punt as early as the Old Kingdom. Extensively used in perfume production, myrrh was the main ingredient in Mendesian and Metopion perfumes and a component of Megaleion, Susinon and Kyphi. Myrrh's sweetness and strength were legendary, and even the birds which flew to Egypt from Punt were said to smell of it! As one of the Seven Sacred Oils it was used to scent the skin and hair of both humans and gods. The resin was referred to as the 'tears of Horus' and was used as an incense; during his reign Rameses III donated almost a ton of it to various temples. Myrrh was an ingredient of face masks, mouthwashes and medicines including headache remedies, soothing massage oils and ointments to treat sores or swollen legs. It was also used as a preservative in wine and in the mummification process.

PISTACIA (*sen-netcher*), often referred to as mastic or terebinth, is a pale yellow gum resin obtained from the Pistacia trees that grew wild in the Egyptian deserts. It was also imported from Punt and the Mediterranean, and imported trees were planted in temple gardens. Traces of pistacia dating back to the Middle Kingdom were found at Memphis and Dahshur. In the New Kingdom, it was used for making incense and perfume, as it still is in the Eastern Desert of Egypt today. In Amenhotep III's palace at Malkata pistacia resin had been added to wine to make an Egyptian version of Retsina.

PRODUCTION

᷸ OILS ᷸

Oil production began with harvesting the various crops from which the oils were extracted: the fruits, seeds and roots were gathered throughout the year and were stored in a cool dry place prior to processing. Several Late Period reliefs portray women gathering raw materials for making perfumed oil. After the plant material was cleaned, any debris was removed by winnowing, after which soaking, drying and rubbing removed any outer casings. Once this was completed the material would be crushed on a slate palette or in a pestle and mortar. The resulting pulp was then pressed to expel the oil.

This was generally done by the expression method, which involved placing the pulverized material inside a cloth or bag, which was then squeezed tourniquet-fashion using wooden poles at either end in order to express the maximum amount of oil; this was then collected in a large pot underneath. This basic technique, still used in parts of southern Europe until early this century, is depicted in tomb scenes dating from the Old Kingdom to the Late Period. A scene in the Middle Kingdom tomb of the nobleman Bakt III at Beni Hasan (*c*.2000 BC) shows a scented ointment being produced using a more sophisticated form of wooden press.

Alternatively, the pulp could be mixed with water and heated until the oil floated to the surface to be skimmed off and collected, a technique still used by the Egyptian Bedouin. The ancient title 'Oil Boiler' (*pes segnen*) uses the hieroglyphic symbol for fire to denote the production process, which is clearly described in an ancient recipe for producing fenugreek oil (*c*.1500 BC):

> Take a great quantity of fenugreek, about two sacks full. Bruise it and leave it in the sun. When completely dry, thresh it like grain, then winnow it until only the pods remain. Everything that has come out of it must be measured and sifted. Divide it into two portions, one consisting of the seeds, the other of the pods of equal quantity. Combine the two portions in water and set aside. Make it into a dough and place

it in a clean pot over the fire. Cook it thoroughly until the moisture has evaporated and it dries up completely with no moisture at all. Remove it from the fire. When it has cooled, place it in another pot and wash it in the river. Wash it thoroughly, making sure it is washed enough by tasting the water in the pot until there is no bitter taste left. Then leave it in the sun spread out on a clean linen cloth. When it is dry, grind it on a millstone, then mix it with water to make a soft dough. Place this in a pot over the fire and cook thoroughly, making sure it boils. It is ready when pellets of oil rise to the surface. Skim off the oil which has risen, straining it through a linen cloth into a clay-lined jar. Then place the oil in an alabaster jar.

These relatively simple methods are similar to culinary techniques and use some of the same equipment, suggesting that oil production could have been carried out on a domestic as well as an industrial level. Nevertheless, a certain amount of expertise would have been required, since some plants are toxic and can cause allergic reactions if not handled carefully. Different production techniques also produce different qualities of oil: for example, cold-pressed poppy seeds produce a yellow oil with a pleasant smell and taste for culinary and perfume use, whereas heat extraction

TO SWEETEN LARD

◆

In a modern version of this process, herbalist Christopher Hedley uses solid vegetable lard instead of animal fat. The 'fatty' odour is removed using wine.

◆

Vegetable lard has already been clarified but usually comes in grains covered with rice flour to stop them sticking together. To remove the rice flour, put the lard in a pan with several times its own volume of water and heat until it melts. Allow to cool. The lard will set on top and the rice flour will have fallen to the bottom and become a paste with the water. Remove the lard. To clear it of its fatty smell put it into a pan with about twice its own volume of sweet wine. Heat gently. The wine will evaporate through the lard which will become impregnated with the sweet smell.
If you smell burning, the wine has completely evaporated, so remove from the heat instantly.
It is best not to allow this to happen!

results in a darker oil with an unpleasant smell, more suited to industrial use. In addition, any contact with copper implements would cause the oils to quickly turn rancid, which is also true of animal fats.

Animal fats were a by-product of the butchery process. They could be extracted in two ways: by using dry heat to melt the fat, then pouring it into cold water to solidify, or by boiling animal parts in water and skimming off the fat from the surface. However, before they could be used in perfume manufacture the characteristic odours of both animal fats and some of the stronger vegetable oils had to be neutralized by adding wine and/or wine-soaked plant materials (such as cyperus or coriander) which were then removed before the final scents could be added. The result-ing oils and fats were referred to as 'sweet' and were then ready to make the perfumes used in cosmetic and medical preparations, temple ritual and mummification.

⌇ PERFUMES ⌇

Ancient Egyptian perfumes were produced by combining these prepared oils and fats with flowers, herbs, spices, aro-matic woods and resins. The distillation process does not seem to have been used until the fourth century BC, before which perfume production generally involved soaking or steeping the required scented materials in the prepared oil or fat which would then absorb their fragrance.

The simplest method, cold steeping (*enfleurage*), was most suitable for floral perfumes derived from petals and

Perfume manufacture. Tomb of an unnamed official of King Tuthmosis IV. Thebes, New Kingdom.

Two servants filling perfume vessels. Relief from the tomb of Mereruka, Saqqara. Old Kingdom.

leaves. In this process the petals or leaves were spread over a layer of semi-solidified oil or fat and pressed between wooden boards, changing the plant matter every day for up to several weeks until the required strength of scent has been transferred into the oil or fat. Alternatively, the plant matter could simply be steeped in liquid oil: myrtle leaves, for example, were steeped in olive oil which then absorbed their strong scent. Hot steeping (*maceration*) involved heating the scented matter in oil or fat at temperatures of up to 65°C (150°F), then straining it while it was still hot. For example, to produce Cyprinum perfume henna seeds were boiled in olive oil, then crushed and the resulting perfumed oil strained off for use.

SCENTED OIL

To make a scented oil by the cold-steeping method, add 50 g (2 oz) of dried herb to ½ litre (1 pint) of oil and allow it to stand in a sunny place for a month before using.

To make a scented oil using heat, simmer 50g (2 oz) of dried herb in ½ litre (1 pint) of oil for 4 hours over water in a double-boiler, then carefully strain it and allow it to cool.

To obtain a solid unguent rather than a liquid oil, take ½ litre (1 pint) of herbal oil prepared as above, heat it gently and stir in 4 tablespoons of cocoa butter and 50 g (2 oz) of beeswax. Remove it from the heat and beat until it is cool and thick.

Painted scenes in the tomb of an unnamed 'Overseer of the Unguent Manufacturers' who lived during the New Kingdom reign of Tuthmosis IV depict several stages of perfume production, beginning with a man cutting slivers of scented wood with an adze. These slivers are then soaked in wine taken from large storage jars. When the steeping is complete, the wine is strained through a sieve, added to quantities of oil or melted fat and heated. When the mixture has been allowed to cool, the surface oils are skimmed off and mixed with crushed herbs and spices prepared in a pestle and mortar. The resulting paste is then shaped into small balls which are placed in a pot, covered with water and boiled. After cooling, the surface oils are again skimmed off and stored in jars.

Perfume production is also recorded in the extensive texts decorating the walls of the perfume laboratories in the Ptolemaic temples at Dendera and Edfu. By this date the highly lucrative perfume industry also operated on a large-scale commercial level, and at Oxyrynchus there was a 'street of the perfume makers'. However, the centre of perfume production was Alexandria, where the workers employed in the perfume factories of the Canopus district were rigorously checked in case they stole any of the costly ingredients: 'a seal is put on their aprons, they have to wear a mask, and before they are allowed to leave the premises they have to take off all their clothes.' Egyptian perfumes were famous throughout the ancient world for their quality and strength, and required complex blends of numerous ingredients. One of the main concerns of Egyptian perfume makers was to ensure that these ingredients were added at precisely the right moment so they had to be highly skilled in their timings. They also had to be very patient, since one of the ritual blends took 93 days to prepare and one of the Sacred Oils no less than 365 days.

Fragrances today are categorized into a few basic types, all of which have further subdivisions. Each perfume has its own structure and is also made up of different 'notes' – low, middle and top – which describe its depth, character and durability. The skill of the perfume maker is to blend them together correctly. The most immediate top notes of Egyptian perfume blends combined sweet fragrances such as lotus, lily, cinnamon and marjoram with the sharper scents of juniper, cardamom and sweet flag. Strong, long-lasting low notes were provided by the various resins which were also used to fix the other perfume ingredients by reducing the evaporation of their essential oils. The names of a number of Egyptian perfumes have been preserved in the ancient texts and include the Seven Sacred

Oils: Festival Oil; *Hekenu* Oil; *Sefeti* Oil; *Nekhenem* oil; *Tewat* oil; Best Cedar Oil and Best Libyan Oil, in addition to Sweet Myrrh. The names of several more have also been preserved in the writings of the classical authors, and are known by their Greek names: Kyphi, Megaleion, Mendesian, Metopion, Sampsuchum and Sampsuchinon, and Susinon.

KYPHI is probably the most famous Egyptian perfume known today, and unlike the other blends was a wine-based perfume made without oil or fat. It was mainly used in ritual, described as a 'welcome to the gods', able to 'lull to sleep, allay anxieties and brighten dreams'. It was made of 'things that delight most in the night', its multiple ingredients resulting in a wonderful fragrance reminiscent of Christmas pudding! Recipes to make a bulk quantity of Kyphi are engraved on the walls of Edfu and Philae temples:

Take 270 g (9½ oz) each of sweet flag, aromatic rush, pistacia resin, cinnamon, mint (?), aspalathus, total 1.87 kg (4 lb). Grind and sieve. Only the powder is to be used, two-fifths of the total = 756g (26½ lb). Take 270g (9½ oz) each of juniper berries, [a plant as yet unidentified], *peker*-plant and cyperus grass; total 1.08 kg (1¼ lb). Grind. Add this to 2.25 kg (5 lb) wine.

KYPHI

In a modern adaptation of the Kyphi recipe, herbalist Christopher Hedley gives:
200 ml (7 fl oz) tincture of bulrushes; 2 bottles of red wine; 500 g (17½ oz) chopped raisins; 200 g (7 oz) crushed myrrh and poplar berries; 20 g (¾ oz) juniper berries; 20 g (¾ oz) crushed blend of myrrh and frankincense; 100 g (3½ oz) fresh sweet flag root; 100 g (3½ oz) lemon grass or lemon-scented geranium. Put all ingredients in a large screw-top jar and leave to soak for 5 days then strain off scented wine. Mix together 300 g (10½ oz) honey and 120 g (4 oz) crushed frankincense, heating until thickened, then mix together with strained scented wine and store in a screw-top container.

Leave until the next morning. Half the wine will be absorbed by the herbs. The rest is to be discarded. Take 1.8 kg (4 lb) raisins and 2.25 kg (5 lb) oasis wine. Grind together well. Remove the rind and pips of the raisins. Place the rest in a pot with the herbs. Leave for five days. Mix 1.2 kg (2½ lb) frankincense and 3 kg (6½ lb) honey in a vessel. Boil gently until thickened and reduced by a fifth, the total weight being 3.36 kg (7½ lb). Mix with the other ingredients and leave for 5 days. Add to this 1.143 kg (2½ lb) finely ground myrrh, and you will have 10.164 kg (22½ lb) Kyphi.

MEGALEION was one of the most difficult perfumes to make, 'since no others involve the mixture of so many and such costly ingredients'. It was made using balanos oil which had first been boiled for ten days and nights to 'drive off impurities', the oil being most receptive when thoroughly boiled. To this was added a quantity of 'burnt resin' and cinnamon mixed with myrrh that had been pressed for several days.

MENDESIAN was known simply as 'the Egyptian'. Made at the Delta town of Mendes, it was generally held to be the best Egyptian perfume of all. Cleopatra was said to scent her feet with it and it was also popular for export. Mendesian was made using a base of balanos oil mixed with myrrh, resin and cinnamon, although by Ptolemaic times almond oil was used instead of balanos. Its strong scent lasted well on the skin, although it could be diluted by mixing it with sweet wine. It also kept very well – one Greek perfume salesman claimed that his stock of eight-year old Mendesian was even better than the freshly made scent. The fragrance of a modern version has been described as 'aromatic resins with a hint of almond and a top note of cinnamon'.

METOPION was named after the Egyptian name for the Sulphur Wort plant from which galbanum resin is derived. It was made of an almond and olive oil base with sweet flag, cardamom, honey, myrrh, balsamum seeds, galbanum and pistacia resin and wine; the best mixture smelt predominantly of cardamom and myrrh rather than of the musky galbanum. A modern recreation of Metopion has been described as 'a mysterious scent, warm and rich, and reminiscent of ripe exotic fruit and spice'.

SAMPSUCHUM was named after the Egyptian name for marjoram, *Semsobek*, literally the 'herb of (the crocodile god) Sobek'. It was made with 500 g (1 lb) bull's fat and 750 g (1½ lb) carefully bruised marjoram, thoroughly mixed together and sprinkled with wine. This was then shaped into small cakes which were placed in a vessel and left overnight. The next day water was poured over them and the mixture gently boiled, then the contents were strained off and left overnight to cool. Another 750 g (1½ lb) marjoram was added to the resulting paste and the boiling and straining process repeated to produce the finished unguent, which was then stored in a cool place. Sampsuchinon oil was also made predominantly of marjoram, 'blackish green and with a sharp, strong scent', to which was added thyme, cinnamon, myrtle leaves, southernwood and nasturtium flowers, 'as much of each as you consider to give a good balance'. These were beaten together and just covered in olive oil, taking care not to add too much, as this would overpower the delicate fragrance of the herbs. This mixture was left to steep for four days then strained and the process repeated with fresh herbs. This produced a 'warming oil best used with honey'.

SAMPSUCHINON

◆

To make a modern version, take dried herbs and grind them to a powder, mix them with enough almond oil to make a paste and simmer the mixture with honey. Cool and place in a pot.

SUSINON was a strongly scented lily oil. The version made in Egypt was 'thought to excel most' by the Greeks, and was used by Cleopatra VII to scent the sails of her royal barge. In a number of Late Period relief scenes the perfume is produced exclusively by women, perhaps using this labour-intensive recipe given by Dioscorides:

Mix 4.2 kg (9 lb 5 oz) oil, 235 g (5 lb 3 oz) sweet flag and 140 g (5 oz) myrrh in scented wine. Boil together and strain. Bruise and macerate 1.6 kg (3 lb 6 oz) cardamom in rain water, and add to oil. Leave to macerate then strain. Take 1,000 lilies, strip them of outer leaves and place in shallow vessel. Pour over 1.6 kg (3 lb 6 oz) oil. Anoint hands with honey and use to stir contents of pot. Leave for 24 hours. Strain and skim oil off water. No water must remain with oil. Take another vessel and smear inside with honey. Pour in oil and sprinkle with salt, removing any impurities as they gather. Set this batch of oil aside. Take the herbs in the sieve and place them in a vessel. Add another 1.6 kg (3 lb 6 oz) oil and 35 g (1¼ oz) crushed cardamom, stir with hands, leave for a while and strain then set aside. Pour remaining oil over plants and repeat with cardamom and salt then set this batch aside. Then take another 1,000 lilies, strip leaves

SUSINON

In a modern and rather more manageable adaptation, herbalist Christopher Hedley gives instructions for a similarly floral-scented unguent using 'sweetened' vegetable lard.

Having sweetened 250 g (9 oz) lard (see p.26), take 100 g (3½ oz) fresh sweet flag root, 10 g (¼ oz) powdered myrrh and 300 ml (10 fl oz) wine. Boil together until the wine has evaporated, allow to cool and skim off the lard. Soak 100 g (3½ oz) crushed cardamom in spring water overnight and add it to the lard. Take 100 g (3½ oz) chopped sweet smelling flowers such as lilies, and add 2 dessertspoons of honey, mix well together and add to the lard. Heat gently in a water bath for two hours. Strain the molten lard through a cloth or fine tea strainer. If the smell is strong enough proceed to the next stage. If not add more flowers and heat again. When you are satisfied with the smell, set the scented lard aside. Next take 10 g (¼ oz) powdered myrrh and 10 g (¼ oz) powdered cinnamon, soak in 60 ml (2 fl oz) spring water overnight and add the scented water to the lard. Heat gently, until the lard has melted. Allow to cool and skim the lard off. Make sure it is completely dry. Store in jars with tight-fitting lids in a cool dark place.

and pour over first batch of oil, repeating with cardamom and salt as before. The more times this is repeated with fresh lilies the stronger the ointment will be. When required strength is obtained take 255 g (9 oz) best myrrh, 35 g (1¼ oz) crocus and 265 g (9⅜ oz) cinnamon. Beat and sift it, place in a vessel with water and pour on a batch of lily-scented oil. Leave for a while, skim off oil, and store in small pots, the insides of which have been coated with gum or myrrh, and saffron and honey diluted with water. Repeat with the second and third batch.

STORAGE

Although pots were used as functional containers, perfumes were also stored in jars of 'alabaster' (calcite), a material considered most suitable for this purpose by the classical authors. Some jars retain traces of their original contents dating back to Predynastic times, and although the excavators generally refer to their 'coconut-like' smell this does not reflect their original fragrance, since the oils and fats have undergone chemical changes over time. However, scientific techniques can now be used to analyze the contents in order to try and work out the actual ingredients. Such an analysis of Predynastic perfumes found at Ballas revealed the contents to be made up of 88% 'fatty matter of vegetable origin', 10% 'dark, possibly coniferous, resin', 1% lime and 1% water. The still soft perfumes in Tutankhamun's tomb consisted of 90% animal fat and 10% resin; one jar was labelled as 'conifer resin', others still had perfume visible around the rim and some even bore the finger prints of the ancient tomb robbers who scooped out and stole their expensive contents. Other pots have yielded traces of the moringa oil, myrrh, frankincense, cinnamon, henna and wine listed in the ancient texts.

Quite a number of perfume and cosmetic jars are also labelled with their contents and capacity: jars from the tomb of Queen MeryetAmun were labelled 'Resinous Oil, 5 hin' (3 litres/5 pints). The three foreign wives of Tuthmosis III, Menhet, Menwi and Merti, were buried with at least ten alabaster pots each, the largest containing 6.5 hin and the smallest 3.5 hin of oily cleansing cream.

Tutankhamun was buried with an amazing 350 litres (77 gallons) of perfume in no fewer than thirty-five alabaster vessels of various shapes and sizes; although most were stoppered with reed bungs, others have more ornate lids featuring gods, animals and heraldic devices.

Smaller perfume vessels were also made of limestone carved into lotus flowers, or carnelian and amethyst embellished with a golden rims. Tutankhamun had a perfume container made of gold set with precious stones, and silver vessels were also used, silver being rarer than gold and therefore more valuable. However, most perfume containers were made of less costly materials, particularly highly glazed faience ware. Stunning vessels of yellow and red faience were made alongside the more familiar blue wares in the workshops of King Amenhotep III attached to his palace at Malkata: some containers bear the royal name, which suggests that they were handed out to courtiers as gifts from the royal family at festivals and court functions.

FROM LEFT TO RIGHT: Alabaster (calcite) vessels. Abu Roash. Old Kingdom. (Leiden Rijksmuseum); Decorative alabaster (calcite) perfume jar. Tomb of Tutankhamun, Valley of the Kings, Thebes. New Kingdom. (Cairo Museum); Alabaster (calcite) jar of cleansing cream belonging to Menhet, Menwi and Merti, the three foreign wives of Tuthmosis III. Valley of the Queens. New Kingdom. (Metropolitan Museum of Art, New York); Yellow faience perfume vessel decorated with the names of King Amenhotep III and his queen Tiye. Malkata, Thebes. New Kingdom. (Louvre, Paris); Glass tilapia fish perfume bottle. Amarna. New Kingdom. (British Museum)

Glass perfume containers were also in use by the New Kingdom, the predominantly blue and yellow colours again worked into a variety of forms from the functional flask and narrow tube shapes to rather more ornate examples such as an open-mouthed glass fish from Amarna. Feline forms were also popular: the name of the cat goddess Bastet was written with the hieroglyph sign representing an alabaster perfume jar (*bas*) and meant 'She of the Perfume Jar'. Wood was also a common material and

LEFT: Turquoise and blue glass perfume bottle. New Kingdom. (Hull Museums)

FAR LEFT: Mixing dish in the form of an antelope. New Kingdom. (British Museum)

BELOW: Floral form spoon. From Memphis (?). New Kingdom. (British Museum)

OPPOSITE: Swimming girl spoon. New Kingdom. (British Museum)

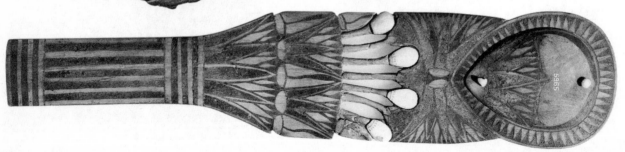

wooden containers often took the form of servant figures carrying pots.

In addition to the vessels used to store and transport prepared perfumes and cosmetics, other types of containers were used to hold smaller quantities and to prepare and mix ingredients. Usually made of wood or ivory, and shaped into naturalistic forms – floral, human or animal – they include shallow dishes and spoon-type implements. A particularly fine example takes the form of a bunch of lotus flowers and buds, the stalks forming the handle. There are also the so-called 'swimming girl' spoons which combine both human and animal forms; the bowl takes the form of a duck or goose towing a swimming girl whose outstretched body forms the handle.

Such objects were generally kept safe and tidy inside some form of box or basket, and whilst most people kept their perfume jars and oil pots in simple reed baskets the wealthy owned beautifully decorated chests with separate compartments for different items. The cedar chest of the butler Kemuny concealed a drawer to hold his alabaster perfume jars. The inlaid ebony casket of the Middle Kingdom princess SitHathorYunet contained both alabaster jars and jars of obsidian edged with gold; being of the wealthiest class she was one of the few who could afford a complete set of Sacred Oils. New Kingdom examples include the cosmetic box of the Royal Architect Kha, which held amongst other things an alabaster pot of hair ointment, while the cosmetic chest of the lady Tutu, wife of the royal scribe Ani, also contained alabaster vessels with their original contents. These boxes are often portrayed in tomb scenes beneath the owners' chair, ensuring the oils and perfumes were close at hand and ready for use throughout eternity.

USES

ᴡ DOMESTIC ᴡ

Both oils and perfumes had a multitude of practical uses in day to day living. Then as now, insects proliferated in Egypt's hot climate and insect repellents were very much in demand. Neat moringa oil was used to prevent mosquito bites, while the galbanum recommended in the ancient texts is still used in the Middle East to treat insect stings and bites. The scent of cedar wafting through cedarwood structures would also have acted as an insect deterrent, whilst an application of cat grease about the house was believed to repel mice.

Inside the home, oils provided light. Castor and sesame oils were burnt in pottery bowls with floating linen wicks, with salt added to prevent smoking. Sesame oil and animal fats were also used to make candles – which could be scented and dyed red with alkanet – and ritual torches of the kind found in Tutankhamun's tomb burnt a mixture of oils, fats and resins.

Homes were also adorned with fragrant floral arrangements in vases and flower bowls, such as the bronze lotus bowl found at the entrance of the tomb of the vizier Rekhmire, who in life had been very proud of his lotus garden. The Egyptians' passion for their gardens is clear from their art and literature. One love poem states, 'I belong to you like this garden that I planted with flowers and sweet smelling plants.' The sweet perfume of flowers would also have been appreciated – 'all the good things

Bronze lotus bowl with Hathor centrepiece. From the entrance to the tomb of Rekhmire, Thebes. New Kingdom.
(Metropolitan Museum of Art, New York)

that sprout from the earth are good things strewn about the house' – although household odours could be neutralized by other means. Ancient texts list 'substances to use in order to make pleasant the smell of the house or clothes: myrrh, frankincense, cyperus – crush, grind, make into one and put on the fire'. One story referred to a house 'scented with incense put on the brazier', whilst a love poem recommended sprinkling cinnamon oil around the bedroom.

∿ SOCIAL ∿

Oils, perfumes and flowers were also an integral part of banquets. The food was prepared using sesame, olive and radish oils, while the aromatic seeds of caraway, coriander and aniseed were added to bread and cakes for their fragrance and digestive qualities. Myrrh and pistacia resins were added to wine for their preservative qualities, and the wine jars were adorned with floral wreaths. Generous quantities of perfume and flowers decorated the room, and guests were encouraged to 'put unguents and perfumes to your nose, and garlands and lotus flowers on the body of your love'.

The entertainers were similarly adorned: singers and dancers alike were 'anointed with myrrh, perfumed with lotus, their heads garlanded with wreaths, fragrant with the plants of Punt, they danced in beauty'. In such a sumptuously fragrant atmosphere the advice in the famous 'Song of the Harpist' was simply to join in – 'Follow your heart as long as you live, put myrrh on your head, anoint yourself with oil fit for a god, heap up your joys and follow your heart, for none are allowed to take their goods with them and none who departs comes back again.'

However, the luxurious Egyptian lifestyle was not to everyone's taste. According to an ancecdote, the Spartan king Agesilaus was so disgusted at the lavish use of perfumes by Egyptian guests at a banquet that he stormed out, thinking them decadent and effeminate. This attitude was the very antithesis of Egyptian customs, where even troops were anointed with perfumes as a mark of honour before setting out on campaign; a letter from one of the army commanders states, 'take heed to have full preparation made in front of Pharaoh, with incense and perfumed oils for the anointing of his soldiers and chariotry.'

In love poetry, 'the woman reclines with her lover, when they are drunken with pomegranate wine and sprinkled with the fragrance of perfumed oil.' Perfume also pervades another, more erotic poem: 'Oh, how I love to bathe before you, allowing you to see my beauty in a dress of finest linen drenched with fragrant unguent...come, look at me!' Given this potency, it is not surprising that perfumed oils were also used in aphrodisiacs and love spells. One particular spell invokes Hathor, the goddess of love, and asks her to send down the power of her father the sun god into a quantity of floral-scented oil. The oil is then mixed with dried fish and a herb associated with Isis; an

Women with lotus flowers. Tomb of Nebamun,
Thebes. New Kingdom. (British Museum)

incantation is spoken over it seven times a day for seven days then it is strained, the fish embalmed with myrrh and natron and buried in secret, and the oil applied to the head of the individual to bring their loved one to them.

Even the act of conception was delicately described in terms of perfume, as the great god Amun sought out the Egyptian queen in the inner rooms of the palace: 'When smelling his divine scent she awoke and smiled at him. At once he proceeded toward her and lusted after her. He gave her his heart. Love for him flowed through her body. The palace became inundated by the scent of the god, it smelt like Punt, the land of incense. Thereupon the god did what he wished, she made him rejoice and she kissed him. She said to him "How splendid it is to see you face-to-face, your dew is through all my limbs!"'

∾ COSMETIC ∾

The main cosmetic function of oils and perfumes was to adorn and enhance the body as part of the toilet routine during which they were applied to both the skin and hair. Pure vegetable oils such as almond were used to cleanse and moisturize the skin, and in the absence of soap, oil and fat mixed with lime or natron (a compound of sodium carbonate and sodium bicarbonate) was used as a form of 'cold cream'; over 30 pots of it were found amongst the cosmetic supplies buried with the three foreign queens of Tuthmosis III.

Among the numerous facial preparations recommended in the ancient medical texts is a 'face wash' of coniferous cedar oil and honey, which can be recreated as follows:

A FACE WASH

◆

Dissolve 1 teaspoon of honey in 6 teaspoons of hot water and mix with fine oatmeal and 4 drops of cedar oil to form a paste.

Other exfoliating-type mixtures include a recipe for 'beautifying the face' – 'take one measure of powdered alabaster, one measure of natron, one measure of northern salt and one measure of warmed honey, grind to a paste and apply'. Another 'for transforming the skin' recommends, 'take one measure of warmed honey, one measure of natron, one measure of northern salt, blend together and anoint' – a modern version using warm honey mixed with coarse salt would do much the same job.

Fragrant oils were also used in the eternal quest to

FOR OILY SKIN

◆

For oily skins use a blend of 2 drops each of cedar and juniper oils in 6 teaspoons of almond or safflower oil – both cedar and juniper were valued for their astringent properties, while almond and safflower oil are recommended in the ancient texts for treating oily skin and spots.

remove signs of ageing. The most famous recipe was a rejuvenating oil made of fenugreek entitled 'The instructions to make an old man into a young man'. It was said to 'remove wrinkles from the face and when it is rubbed into the skin it is left beautiful; it removes blemishes, disfigurements, all signs of age and all weaknesses and has been found effective a million times.'

Another popular recipe designed to 'expel wrinkles from the face' lists 'one measure of frankincense oil, one measure of wax, one measure of fresh moringa oil and one measure of cyperus grass ground finely, mix with fermented plant juice or oil and apply daily. Make it and you will see!' This mixture would have had some success, since

A REMEDY FOR AGEING SKIN

◆

For a modern variation gently heat 1½ tablespoons
of beeswax and 1 tablespoon of white wax together
and slowly add 80 ml (3 fl oz) almond or safflower oil.
Warm 2 tablespoons of distilled water separately and
dissolve ½ teaspoon of borax in it, add 2 tablespoons
of rosewater and mix into the warm wax and oil.
Beat together until cooled to room temperature,
add 4 drops of frankincense oil and beat again
until blended.

FOR DRY AND MATURE SKIN

◆

Dry and mature skins also benefit from
a simple blend of 2 drops each of frankincense
and galbanum oils in 6 teaspoons of almond oil;
for a rich night-time version add 2 drops
each of frankincense and myrrh oils to
6 teaspoons of wheatgerm oil.

frankincense is used effectively today in modern aromatherapy in tackling ageing skin.

The ancient Egyptians also used face packs, particularly
a moisturizing blend of 'frankincense, honey and grain
made into as dough and pounded with water and applied
to the face often'. This is almost identical to modern oat-
meal-based packs in which fine oatmeal is blended with a
little water and almond oil, mixed with warmed honey and
a few drops of frankincense oil and applied to the face for
five minutes once a week. The same mixture can be used
for oily skins, substituting cedar oil for the frankincense; an
oily complexion might also benefit from an ancient face
pack based on egg-white and acacia flowers; for a modern
variation, whip together two egg whites and place in a
blender with a peeled, chopped cucumber.

Oil-based cosmetics were used to enhance the appearance further; the distinctive black eyepaint kohl made of
powdered galena (lead ore) was often mixed with oil or fat
for a thicker consistency. Judging from the distinctly rosy
complexions found in a number of New Kingdom scenes,
women in particular liked to enhance their lips and cheeks
with rouge made from powdered red ochre mixed with oil,
fat or gum resin. To 'make the smell of the mouth agree-
able' they used a mixture of myrrh, frankincense and cype-

rus, crushed and mixed with honey produced what must have been the world's first breath-freshening chewing gum!

The Egyptians' crowning glory however, was surely their hair, both real and false. Wigs and false braids were extremely popular for both men and women and they often stored these with chips of aromatic wood. Analysis of a wig in the British Museum has revealed that its style was held in place by a fragrant setting-lotion of beeswax and resin. Problems with the natural hair could also be dealt with using oils and perfumed materials: a complex dandruff remedy advised 'five measures of ground roasted barley and five measures of soft grease, mix together and anoint the head; follow this with fish oil on the second day, hippopotamus fat on the third day and ladanum resin on the fourth day'. The use of such oily concoctions would seem to be based on their ability to moisturize a dry scalp, and to this day fish oil is prescribed as an internal remedy for the same problem. Greying hair could be dyed with a plant-based mixture containing juniper berries mashed in oil and heated; it has been noted that the natural colouring matter in the plants would stain the hair whilst the astringent qualities of the juniper would stimulate the scalp.

Baldness remedies proliferate in the ancient texts, the most famous being a hair restorer made of date kernels, donkey hoof and dog's paw boiled in oil and rubbed on the scalp. Alternatively, one could 'rub the head of the bald one with a mixture of fat of the lion, hippopotamus, crocodile, cat, snake and goat.' Another version was based on hedgehog fat, possibly through association with the creature's fine collection of bristles! The therapeutic effect of cedar on both the hair and the scalp has long been known, and a rather more pleasant remedy using cedar and vegetable oils can be made according to the following recipe:

A REMEDY FOR BALDNESS

◆

Mix together 2 tablespoons of almond oil, 1 teaspoon of olive oil and 20 drops of cedar oil. Rub gently on the scalp a few hours before shampooing. Alternatively, 15 drops of cedar oil can simply be added to one's regular bottle of shampoo.

Castor oil is another long-prized ingredient in hair treatments, and was prescribed in ancient times to 'cause the hair of a woman to grow. The woman shall rub her head with it'. Body hair could also be removed using a depilatory lotion of gum resin, sycamore sap, cucumber, boiled crushed bird-bones and fly dung.

Hair was in fact regarded as highly erotic, and its seductive qualities were enhanced even further by the lavish use of perfume. Ancient tales of its effects abound: in one New Kingdom story, a perfumed lock of hair which falls into the royal laundry scents the pharaoh's clothing, causing him to fall in love with its equally fragrant owner. In a love poem of similar date a woman exclaims 'my hair is weighed down with perfume', while in the Roman poem 'The Lock of Berenice' the Ptolemaic queen offers a lock of her fragrant hair to the gods. The hair of Hathor, goddess of love and beauty, was described as 'sweet and perfumed', while the priestesses of Isis had 'locks moist with perfume'. Men also scented their hair, and tomb scenes dating back to the Old Kingdom show the hair of noblemen being dressed with liquid perfume; soldiers and workmen alike used oils of various kinds, and young male city dwellers were described as wearing 'sweet oil upon their heads'.

Oily hair ointments made of lotus, myrrh, cumin and juniper in moringa oil helped to keep both hair and scalp in good condition in Egypt's hot, dry climate. The most important part of the body care routine was a daily appli-

cation of oils to protect the skin and hair from the sun.

It has long been thought that the hair was treated with an actual lump or cone of moisturizing cream placed on top of the head, an object which appears in painting and relief scenes from the late Middle Kingdom to the early Ptolemaic period. These 'cones' were supposed to have melted slowly, releasing their scent over the head and upper body – always assuming of course that they could be successfully balanced on top of the head! Considering the Egyptians' meticulous attention to their appearance, the time they spent bathing and having their hair and wigs carefully styled, it seems unlikely that they would then sit completely still as warm animal fat slowly trickled down over their carefully made-up faces. It is more likely that the artist was simply making a visual reference to the fact that generous quantities of perfumes had been applied to the hair and scalp, the neat cone shape representing nothing more than an artistic convention. The brown staining on the upper body, so often described as having run down from the head, is simply the result of perfumed oils rubbed on the skin showing through the fine linen garments being worn over the top. The Egyptians very much appreciated the feeling of soft skin which resulted from moisturizing their bodies with fragrant oils.

The use of strongly-scented perfumes on the body was not, however, an attempt to mask poor personal hygiene, since the Egyptians were meticulous in such matters. They were the first people to use deodorants – one deodorant recipe, using carob-pulp pellets rubbed over the body, was entitled 'a remedy to stop smells in a man or a woman'. Another 'remedy to prevent odour in summer' advocated incense and dough mixed together, made into a ball and applied to 'the places where the limbs join', while, as today, henna powder was used to neutralize foot odour. Daily bathing was standard practice for all, in contrast with other ancient people who only ever washed for ritual or festive occasions! Most Egyptians bathed in the Nile, but religious personnel had to bathe twice each day and twice each night in the pure waters of the sacred lakes attached to their temples. Even the king had to undergo ritual purification before entering the temple: the en-suite bathroom of Rameses III can still be seen in the palace attached to his temple at Medinet Habu. In contrast, the baths at Dendera temple were therapeutic and used water previously poured over statues of the goddess Hathor. The ancients also knew the value of the aromatic bath, and lotus and coriander were added to lukewarm water to expel fever.

AROMATIC BATH OIL

Add 5 drops of lotus oil to the bath for a cooling, calming effect or 5 drops of frankincense oil for a sedative, calming effect; alternatively add the oils to a small amount of almond oil, rub this into the skin and allow a warm shower to release the fragrance.

ꙮ THERAPEUTIC ꙮ

The Egyptians suffered from the usual aches and pains and dealt with them using massage to relax tense muscles, calm the nerves, stimulate the circulation and clean toxins from the body. It is clear from their art and literature that massage was practised from the earliest times: one story relates how the elderly Djedi, magician to the court of King Cheops, spent his days at home, 'lying on a mat in the courtyard of his house', while servants anointed and massaged him – no doubt to ease his elderly joints, since he was said to be no less than 110 years old!

The benefits of massage with a base oil such as almond or castor oil were then as now enhanced by the addition of perfume – 3 drops of fragrant oil to 1 teaspoon of base oil as an approximate guide – the specific oils used depending not only on wealth but also on personal preference and the therapeutic or magical effects required. Medical texts give separate remedies for the head, back, joints, limbs, thighs, front of the shin and feet and so on, and listing the relative qualities of different blends – soothing, invigorating, rejuvenating, stimulating and so forth. The addition of perfume also represents the beginnings of aromatherapy, which recognizes that each fragrance has its own specific properties. Most recipes were for 'soothing' blends, the Wisdom Texts stating that 'ointment is soothing for the body'. The recommended 'frankincense and cinnamon in moringa oil' would have been particularly efficacious since frankincense is soothing. It also blends particularly well with cinnamon, although another recipe 'to treat stiff limbs' suggests an oil containing frankincense and myrtle.

To keep the body supple, castor oil was the most commonly used since it was the cheapest; when mixed with honey it was rubbed into the skin to ease 'pains in all limbs'. Other blends to promote suppleness involved the use of frankincense, myrrh and honey in almond oil: the longest remedy in the Ebers Medical Papyrus is a massage lotion containing no less than thirty-seven ingredients including myrrh, 'herbs of the field', cyperus, fennel, barley, flax, natron, resin, lotus resin, sycamore resin, white oil, goose fat, bull's fat and the scented wood chips from cedar, mulberry, willow and sycamore. Another recipe gives 'honey and fish oil blended with the yeast of sweet beer', an ancient form of Brewer's Yeast, which is known to be of tremendous benefit to the skin, nourishing it while drawing out impurities to leave a tingling, stimulating feeling. Olive oil was said to 'make the body ready for the performance of actions', while the Sacred Oils were also thought to 'reinvigorate the limbs'.

MASSAGE OIL

◆

A blend to ease stiffness: mix 6 drops of frankincense oil in 2 teaspoons of almond oil.
A blend to keep the body supple: mix 2 tablespoons of castor oil with 1 tablespoon of almond oil.

Whilst both lotus and myrrh oils were cooling, others would have had a mollifying effect, particularly Metopion and Sampsuchinon, the latter described as a 'warming oil best used with honey'. A vigorous massage with almond or juniper oil to induce perspiration was felt to be the best way to alleviate fever, and a hot oil massage using wormwood and herbs was recommended to bring out body heat before a fever broke. Medical texts also advised the practitioner to 'fumigate the man with myrtle, quench it with sweet beer to cause him to perspire, then massage him with your hand', such massages generally being followed by a warm bath and sleep.

It is also apparent that the Egyptians took great care of their feet, and ancient Egypt also provides the earliest evidence of reflexology, the healing art which uses pressure on certain points of the feet to produce a highly effective and relaxing treatment. Relief scenes in the Old Kingdom temple of King Niuserre depict courtiers holding an oil pot and massaging the royal feet, and similar scenes in the contemporary Saqqara tomb reliefs of Ptahhotep show the tomb owner seated while a servant massages his feet and ankles. The tombs of Khentika and Ankhmahor even show the same manipulation of the hands and feet found in modern reflexology, the accompanying comments of those involved conveying the therapeutic benefits of the treatment: 'Make this pleasant, dear one', 'Give them strength', 'Do not cause pain in these', and so on.

In the story of the elderly royal magician Djedi, he is described as lying on a mat to have his feet rubbed by a servant, and in a New Kingdom love poem a woman takes the garlands from the neck of her drunken lover and lies him on a bed before stroking and rubbing his feet. Cleopatra VII was said to use Mendesian perfume purely on her feet, a trend adopted by wealthy Greeks who used this rich

Massage and reflexology scenes from the tomb
of Khentika, Saqqara. Old Kingdom. (After James 1953)

Egyptian unguent 'to steep their feet and legs'. One of the main ingredients in Mendesian is cinnamon, which was felt especially beneficial to aching feet. Cedar was recommended in the ancient texts to deal with swollen feet, either mixed with acacia leaves and honey or fat, or with fresh dates in a myrrh and wax mixture.

TO EASE ACHING FEET

◆

Add 3 drops of cinnamon oil to 1 teaspoon of almond oil and rub the blend into the feet; alternatively, 4 drops of cinnamon oil can be added to a warm footbath (as can 4 drops each of thyme and chamomile, or indeed cedar, with similar results).

Galbanum was another ancient remedy for aching feet and wormwood was used in a soothing foot cream worn by travellers against fatigue and to stimulate the circulation. When rubbed or massaged into the feet such fragrant blends would have proved extremely beneficial, especially for those walking long distances; in the case of soldiers covering long distances on campaign, immobilization was a very serious matter, and there are in fact a number of relief scenes showing army encampments in which soldiers are having their feet massaged. In cases where their feet had been blistered or cut, they would have been taken care of by army physicians, and in one New Kingdom story the feet of a prince who has travelled a great distance are washed and examined, anointed and bandaged with some kind of poultice. This mixture was no doubt similar to the honey and plant oil mixtures listed in the medical texts and sent ready-prepared to Egyptian fortresses in Nubia. One poultice for 'diseased toes' involved a mixture of fennel, wax, frankincense, cyperus, wormwood, myrrh, poppy seeds, elderberries, resin, cedar oil, olive oil and 'water from the rains of heaven'.

∾ MEDICINAL ∾

The majority of Egyptian medicines were made up of plant materials, and many of their medical remedies have parallels with today's herbal medicine. Herbal remedies were designed to be taken internally by swallowing or inhaling, or externally by application to the body. In the opinion of Homer, 'the fertile soil of Egypt is most rich in herbs, many of which are wholesome in solution, and in medical knowledge the Egyptian leaves the rest of the 'world behind' – thus it was an Egyptian woman, Polydamna, who taught the medicinal arts to Helen of Troy. Another Greek writer, Theophrastus, noted the beneficial effects of perfume in this context: 'It is to be expected that perfumes should have medicinal properties in view of the virtues of their spices. The effect of plasters and poultices prove these virtues, since they disperse tumours and abscesses and produce a distinct effect on the body and its interior parts. If one lays perfume on his abdomen or breast he produces fragrant odours on his breath.'

The recipes given in the ancient texts housed in temple libraries would have been made up by specially trained individuals and stored in containers, which like the perfume jars were often inscribed with their contents and instructions for use. Household remedies would simply be passed down through families by word of mouth, and like oils and perfumes would have been made up at home using approximate measures. General pain relief relied on a preparation of linseed oil or myrtle mixed with honey and flour, but there was a whole range of specific remedies – ranging from the sophisticated to the downright bizarre – intended to deal with the particular diseases and problems associated with each part of the body.

Eye complaints caused by the heat, flies and wind-blown sand were common, and were generally treated using a kohl-based mixture blended with gum or lettuce oil. Other eye medicines relied on carob pulp and honey; one container, labelled 'very good eye-salve for inflammation of the eyes' came with instructions that it was to be used between specific dates and seasons, presumably times when different eye diseases were prevalent.

Headaches also seem to have been common, and again this could be put down largely to the excessive heat. One remedy, said to have been prepared by the goddess Isis to cure the headache of the sun god Ra, advised the sufferer to 'take equal parts of juniper, coriander, poppy, wormwood and honey. Mix to a paste and smear on the head to instantly become well'. Other ancient headache remedies which feature the beneficial effects of juniper

A REMEDY FOR HEADACHES

Juniper and coriander are frequently used in modern headache remedies. Try 1 drop of each added to 1 teaspoon of almond oil. Massage into the temples and around the back of the neck.

included a mixture of cumin, myrrh, lotus and juniper in moringa oil, and ladanum, frankincense, juniper, kohl and red ochre added to ibex fat.

Earache was generally treated with oils, as it is today; ear drops of lettuce oil and ladanum were poured into the ear to treat 'purulence' and a marjoram and hyssop earache mixture is paralleled in modern aromatherapy, where warmed almond oil and marjoram is used. Toothache remedies relied on carob pulp, cumin and frankincense, while teething pains in young children were dealt with using a recipe of poppy seeds and fly dung mixed in water and drunk, the narcotic effect of the poppy seeds possibly proving more effective than the other ingredient!

Cures for respiratory problems – again caused in part by the environment – included liquid cough mixtures of myrtle, lettuce and beer, acacia, honey and beer, or cumin, honey and milk. Asthma was also treated with a wine-based mixture of fruit, juniper, cumin and frankincense: the use of cumin regulated the metabolic processes of the body and frankincense is still regarded as excellent in treating respiratory problems in general and asthma in particular.

Stomach aches similarly relied on the remedial powers of frankincense, blended with honey, moringa oil and wine, whilst specifically female complaints were treated with either Susinon lily oil or Sampsuchinon oil, the marjoram, thyme and myrtle used in Sampsuchinon's preparation still prescribed for problems relating to both the menstrual cycle and to childbirth.

Skin problems were largely treated with oils, particularly castor oil: 'a person who suffers from skin disease…will be like someone to whom nothing has happened. He shall be anointed for 10 days early, so that the disease goes away. Really efficient, tried a million times.' Radish oil could also be used, while moringa oil was recommended for skin inflammations, particularly in a remedy containing alkanet, carob and resin. Burn scars could be treated with honey mixed with either frankincense or carob pulp; alternatively, a mixture of barley bread, salt and oil was recommended 'for an immediate cure, really excellent, I have seen it occur wonderfully'. Wounds were dressed with a cedar unguent or Metopion perfume, whose myrrh and galbanum ingredients were invaluable for such purposes. A carob and frankincense unguent was also applied to dry up wounds, and sores were treated with coriander and honey.

Oils were also used against insects and parasites: neat safflower oil was applied to insect bites, while snake bites were treated with coriander. Coriander seeds were also used against internal parasites. Oils were particularly effective in dealing with headlice: a daily application of moringa oil, castor oil and fat is recommended by the ancient texts to remove 'that which moves about on the head'. In more recent times both Nubians and the inhabitants of Siwa Oasis have used oil for this purpose, and modern research has revealed that oil actually does reduce the lice's movement through the hair, reducing their uptake of oxygen and suffocating them!

Should all else fail, magic was used to combat the hidden forces which must have caused the problems: bryony was burnt as a fumigant to expel demonic disease and flowers were used in incantations to 'cleanse everything from pestilence' whilst invoking the gods.

～ RELIGIOUS ～

The gods who watched over Egypt were imagined 'clothed in red linen and anointed with fine oil'. As the most fragrant beings imaginable, wherever they went was 'inundated by the divine scent'. Many deities were also associated with a specific fragrance which could be used in rituals to invoke them.

Nefertum was the young god of the primeval lotus. His name meant 'perfection' and he was generally portrayed in human form with a huge lotus flower crown or as a small child crouched on a lotus flower. He was regarded as the scented blue lotus out of which the sun rose, and the 'lotus blossom at the nose of [the sun god] Ra'. In tomb and temple scenes the fragrance of the lotus is inhaled by royalty and courtiers alike; its scent was regarded as protective as well as restorative, since Nefertem was regarded as the 'protector of the two lands'.

Nefertem's mother was the cat goddess Bastet whose name is written with the hieroglyph sign of a sealed alabaster perfume jar (*bas*) and meaning 'She of the Perfume Jar'; whilst this might represent the ritual purity involved in

Serpentine perfume vessel with lion. Leontopolis. Late Period. (Brooklyn Museum)

her cult, it could be that as mother of the lotus god, she was literally regarded as the sacred vessel which carried the lotus! Indeed, perfume vessels were sometimes carved in feline form, a small alabaster wildcat representing the goddess' grace and strength. Royal perfume jars feature lions and are comparable to examples from Leontopolis, the 'city of the lion'. Originally interpreted as simply a kind of heraldic representation of the city, the feline motif could also refer to the cult centre of Bastet at nearby Bubastis.

Other gods also had their own fragrances. Marjoram was sacred to Sobek, the fearsome crocodile god who symbolized the power of the king and was said 'to make the herbage green'. Known to classical writers as Sampsuchum, its Egyptian name was *semsobek* ('the herb of Sobek'). The lettuce was symbolic of Min, ithyphallic god of fertility and 'great of love'; lettuce oil was reputed to have aphrodisiac qualities and promote high fertility in men, and certain priests were forbidden to eat it! The herb Black Horehound was known as the 'blood of Isis', whilst myrrh was referred to as the 'tears of Horus', Isis' son. The young god is very much associated with the ritual use of perfumes and as Horhekenu, literally 'Horus-of-the-Unguent', he was regarded as 'Lord of Protection'.

The little-known deity Merhet was the goddess of embalming oil, while the means of oil and perfume production were embodied by Shesmu, god of the oil press. Originally described as the 'crusher of enemies' he eventually assumed a rather more benign role as producer of oils and perfumes, particularly the fine oil of the sun god Ra, and at Edfu and Dendera temples he was venerated as 'Master of Perfumery'.

The name of the great state god Amun – the 'Hidden One' – also describes the way perfume works. An invisible substance, it can nevertheless and quite inexplicably stir up countless feelings, responses and emotions. If sufficiently intoxicating, it can be used to alter states of consciousness, adding to the magical and mystical aura surrounding the rituals in which the gods were honoured with a constant stream of offerings in the form of fragrant perfumes, incense, flowers and candles in both state temples and household shrines.

Incense – a word derived from the Latin verb *incendere*, 'to burn' – was believed to purify both the worshipped and their worshippers. Its billowing fragrant smoke added to the dramatic impact of temple ritual and was said to sweeten the fragrance of the sanctuary, driving away malevolent spirits while simultaneously attracting the gods down into their cult statues. Drops of perfumed oils, grains of resin, aromatic wood chips, crumbled bark, berries, leaves and flowers were used alone or in blends, often compressed into small balls, cakes and cones, and either thrown on to open flames or burnt on glowing charcoal.

As with perfumes in general, each incense had a specific purpose and effect. Frankincense resin, regarded as 'sustenance for the gods', is still used today by the Egyptian Copts in their churches and homes. Ancient incense recipes used crushed frankincense blended with crushed myrrh, crumbled cinnamon bark or powdered cyperus grass mixed with warm honey and formed into small balls. When mixed with wax, dates and wine frankincense was also used to invoke the god Anubis.

Frankincense was also one of the key ingredients in Kyphi, the wine-based ritual perfume described as a 'welcome to the gods' since it contained so many good things! Although the previously quoted Kyphi recipes produce a liquid perfume, a more solid incense can be made by

Kenna burns incense on a charcoal brazier. Tomb of Inherkha, Thebes. New Kingdom.

adding raisins to a small quantity of wine and leaving them to steep for five days before adding juniper berries, powdered acacia and henna leaves and crushed sweet flag root. Mix them together and leave for twenty-four hours. Grind this mixture in a mortar and add equal parts of it to a powdered mixture of frankincense and pistacia resin, peppermint, bay leaves, hibiscus flowers, cinnamon, orris root and sandalwood. Mix thoroughly together and add powdered myrrh and warmed honey to bind it. Spread it out on a baking sheet until dry, divide into small pieces to burn as required on a charcoal disc. Other combinations of powdered dried herbs and flowers can be combined, using warm honey and gum resins to harden the mixture; alternatively, they can simply be burnt as they are along with cinnamon sticks – vast quantities of cinnamon were listed as temple offerings during the reigns of the New Kingdom pharaohs Hatshepsut, Seti I and Rameses III.

The term *sn-ntr*, meaning 'fragrance of the gods', refers particularly to the pale yellow pistacia resin, traces of which have been found in both homes and temples as far back as 2000 BC. The incense was burnt in small bowls, hand-held burners made in the form of an outstretched human hand and arm or possibly in ritual spoons similar to those used for perfumes. Used at regular intervals throughout the day in an endless cycle of rituals, the incense was followed by the presentation of ritual perfumes (*idet*), and during his reign Rameses III alone offered more than 16,000 jars of perfume to the gods.

Each morning the purified high priest, delegating for the king, entered the small cedar-scented shrine at the very heart of the temple amidst clouds of incense and opened the sealed doors to approach the god's statue, which he would first greet before presenting the perfume. He would then use it to anoint the brow of the god using the little finger of his right hand, a ritual portrayed in a number of temple scenes and referred to in religious texts: 'O Cedar perfume which is on the brow of Horus'. Both cedar and myrrh, as two of the Sacred Oils, were used extensively for this purpose; myrrh was used to anoint the goddesses Hathor and Maat and was referred to as 'an unguent intended for the limbs of Amun'. A Hymn to Amun states that 'the dwellers of Punt come to you, bringing you their perfumes, to make festive your temple with festive fragrance. Incense bearing trees drop incense for you and the perfume of your aroma penetrates the nose, all costly oils come to you and cedar trees are grown for you'.

Royalty were also anointed, since the glistening oil was thought to render the wearer immune to the powers of darkness: Hatshepsut is described with 'the best of myrrh on all her limbs, her fragrance is divine dew, her odour is mingled with Punt, her skin is gilded, shining as do the stars before the whole land'. During the New Year Protection Rituals, the king used lotus oil, which was symbolic of renewal, and both myrrh and lotus were great favourites, particularly amongst the female clergy.

The dark atmospheric interiors of the temples were brightly lit with scented candles and oil lamps: to honour the sun god Ra, Rameses III 'planted olive trees for you equipped with many people who make pure oil in order to light the lamps in your holy dwelling.'

In fact the gardens which provided the temples with their own oils, flowers and herbs date back to at least 2000 BC with the sycamore and tamarisk groves planted by King Montuhotep II at Deir el-Bahari. Following his military campaigns abroad King Tuthmosis III brought back new species to Egypt, the 'plants which his majesty encountered in the land of Syria-Palestine' still to be seen in reliefs at Karnak temple. Certain temples had vast estates and their own gardening staff: the official Nakht, 'Gardener of the Divine Offerings of Amun' under King Amenhotep III, 'planted all kinds of flowers' in the temple gardens at Karnak. However, one high priest actually had to fence off his temple gardens following raids on the temple orchards when 'its shrubs were taken into intruders' homes'! As well as olive trees, Rameses III planted whole groves of incense trees around the temples, along with all the flowers necessary to provide the millions of floral bouquets listed in detail as necessary for temple offerings.

The lotuses, lilies, cornflowers, safflowers and poppies so loved for their beauty and colour were also believed to contain the very essence of the gods themselves, thus bouquets and wreaths were extensively used in worship, piled on altars and stacked around cult statues, a gift of the gods returned back to them in the form of offerings. As Amun himself tells the great King Amenhotep III: 'I made the lands of Punt come here to you with all the fragrant flowers in their lands, to beg your peace and breathe the air you give.' Flowers were also central to religious festivals in which the gods' statues were taken in procession to visit the dead in their tombs. The flowers infused with the divine essence were taken from the temple altars and whilst still full of regenerative perfume presented to the dead.

∾ FUNERARY ∾

Even in death the power of fragrance was held to be of vital importance, and the use of oils and perfumes was as lavish as it had been in daily life, perhaps even more so. The process of mummification itself involved the use of oils and perfumes at every step – oils were believed to 'unite the limbs, join the bones and assemble the flesh' whilst perfumes were used to hide decay and thus deny it.

Those with sufficient means would be artificially mummified, a complex process which took seventy days to complete before the funeral and burial could proceed. In the most traditional and costly form, the internal organs were removed from an incision across the lower body and placed in separate jars containing preservative cedar resin. A cheaper option was to inject the body with a strong cedar oil which would simply dissolve the internal organs away. The body cavity was then washed with an infusion of palm wine and spices before being filled with bruised myrrh, cinnamon and 'every other aromatic substance', following which the incision was sewn up and smeared with resin. Following its complete dehydration in dry natron and juniper berries the body was then washed again and beneath the watchful eye of Merhet, goddess of the embalming oil, the skin of the deceased would be anointed with various oils and resins.

It has been suggested that the translucent golden qualities of the resins linked them to the reviving light of the creator sun god, whilst the glistening oils, considered as deeply protective, were thought to render the wearer immune to the powers of darkness. According to funerary texts, frankincense resin mixed with fat was specifically used to anoint the head, and another text refers to the use of cedar and oils in preparing the body. Classical authors say that the body was anointed with juniper or cedar oil, and cedar, one of the Sacred Oils, was known as 'the preservative of the dead'. Modern research confirms the preservative and antiseptic qualities of cedar and chamomile oils, which had been used in the mummification of Rameses II. Large quantities of scented oils were also used during the mummification of Tutankhamun, the archaeologists estimating that 'two bucketfuls' had been poured over the body! Even non-royal mummies were extensively treated with juniper and cinnamon oils. Following the post-mortem 'massage' the body was generally rubbed with myrrh and cinnamon, both excellent antibacterial preservatives. When the body of priest Natsef-Amun was unwrapped in Leeds in 1828 there was found to be 'a thick layer of spicery covering every part of it, still retaining the faint smell of cinnamon, but when mixed with alcohol or water and exposed to heat the odour of myrrh becomes very powerfully predominant', recalling a passage in an ancient text, 'Death is before me today, like the fragrance of myrrh.'

The Book of the Dead instructed the deceased that in order to pass into the afterlife they had to be pure, clean, 'anointed with the finest oil of myrrh' and clothed in fresh linen, which in death took the form of mummy bandages, linen strips wrapped repeatedly around the body. The sixteen layers of Tutankhamun's bandages were interspersed with antiseptic juniper berries, while those of a later Ptolemaic mummy contained the first ever cotton-wool ball, soaked in myrrh, cinnamon and juniper oil! The wrapped body was then anointed even further and placed inside its nest of body-shaped coffins; these were also anointed, analysis of the now-blackened 'anointing fluids' indicating a mixture of beeswax, galbanum and water.

Once prepared for burial, the body was taken in fra-

'Opening of the Mouth' Ceremony at the funeral of Ani in a scene from his Book of the Dead. New Kingdom. (British Museum)

grant procession to the tomb, both the mourners and the mummy wearing floral collars. The funerary rituals were then performed amidst clouds of incense used to purify both the body and the tomb; the small bowls which contained the frankincense burnt during Tutankhamun's funeral were labelled 'incense for fumigation'. Then, standing the mummy upright within its coffin, the priests would anoint it with Sacred Oil before performing the 'Opening of the Mouth Ceremony' designed to reawaken the senses of the deceased. As the mouth, eyes, ears and nose were symbolically 'reopened' with ritual implements, they were sated with offerings as the standard offering formula was recited: 'a thousand jars of perfume, incense, unguent and all kinds of herbs, all kinds of offerings on which the gods also live'. What better way of reactivating the sense of smell than by anointing the deceased with costly perfumes, enveloping them in clouds of sweet incense and offering them sweet-scented flowers whose fragrance was considered potent enough to restore the dead? After the funeral rites the deceased was then laid to rest within a tomb decorated with offering scenes and provided with as many of the Sacred Oils they could afford, from the single jar of the manual worker to the hundreds of litres found in royal burials.

So, having been given all possible necessities and instructions, the soul of the deceased could then set out to an eternally fragrant afterlife. The Book of the Dead contains the spell to transform it into a lotus flower: 'I am this pure lotus flower that has ascended by the sunlight and is at the nose of the sun god Ra. I am the pure lotus that ascends upwards.' For the Egyptians the opening of the lotus each dawn symbolized the triumph of light over darkness and life over death, the human condition expressed in terms of a single fragrant bloom. A final prayer lists the offerings made to the souls of the dead, the things that every Egyptian loved most: 'Take these lotus flowers and every bloom and every herb of sweet odour at its season, cool water and incense and every offering requirement in full, that you soul may be satisfied with them for ever and ever…'

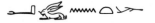

GLOSSARY

ACACIA (*Acacia nilotica*): wood, leaves, white-yellow flowers, pods and gum used in cosmetics and medicine. Astringent.

ALKANET (*Alkanna tinctoria*): plant roots used in medical remedies and for red dye in perfume and candle production. Antiseptic.

ALMOND (*Prunus dulcis*): oil from kernels used in perfume production, medicine and massage. Demulcent, emollient.

ANISEED (*Pimpinella anisum*): plant with oil-producing fruit and seeds used in medicine, massage and cooking. Antiseptic, digestive, stimulant.

BALANOS (*Balanites aegyptiaca*): oil from kernels of tree used as base for perfumes and cosmetics.

BRYONY (*Bryonia dioica*): herb used as incense and in medical remedies. Purgative.

CARDAMOM (*Elettaria cardamomum*): spice used in perfume production and massage. Antiseptic, aphrodisiac, digestive, stimulant.

CAROB (*Ceratonia siliqua*): pods used for cosmetics and medicine. Demulcent, lubricant, vermifuge.

CASTOR OIL PLANT (*Ricinus communis*): plant with oil-producing seeds used in medicine, massage and lighting. Emetic, emollient, lubricant.

CEDAR (*Cedrus libani*): wood, resin and oil used in cosmetic and medical recipes, massage, rituals and mummification. Antiseptic, astringent, emollient, insecticide, sedative.

CHAMOMILE (*Anthemis tinctoria*): plant with flowers and oil-producing seeds used in ritual, medicine, mummification and dyeing. Antiseptic, emollient, insecticide.

CINNAMON (*Cinnamonium zeylanicum*): wood and leaves used in perfumes and incense, medicine, massage and mummification. Antiseptic, aphrodisiac, astringent, insecticide, stimulant.

COLOCYNTH (*Citrullus colocynthus*): ground plant with oil-producing seeds used from earliest times. Purgative.

CORIANDER (*Coriandrum sativum*): herb used in ritual, perfume production, medical and therapeutic remedies, considered aphrodisiac. Digestive, stimulant.

CUMIN (*Cumin cyminum*): seeds used in ritual, medicine and cooking. Antiseptic, aphrodisiac, digestive, stimulant.

CYPERUS (*Cyperus esculentus*): sedge plant with oil-producing tubers and leaves used in perfume and cosmetic preparations.

DATE PALM (*Phoenix dactylifera*): tree with fruit used in wine and perfume production, medicine and mummification.

FENUGREEK (*Trigonella foenum-graecum*): herb used in medical remedies and beauty treatments. Nutritive.

FRANKINCENSE (*Boswellia sp*): gum resin used in incense, perfume production, cosmetic and medical recipes, in massage and mummification. Antiseptic, astringent, digestive, sedative.

GALBANUM (*Peucedanum galbaniflora*): gum resin used in perfume production, medical remedies, massage and mummification. Analgesic, expectorant, sedative, stimulant.

HENNA (*Lawsonia inermis*): shrub with leaves, seeds and flowers used in perfumes, cosmetics, and medical preparations. Astringent.

JUNIPER (*Juniperus phoenicea*): wood and berries used in cosmetic and medical preparations, perfumes and incense, massage and mummification. Antiseptic, diuretic, insecticide, stimulant.

LADANUM (*Cistus spp.*): resin from leaves used as incense and in medical remedies.

LETTUCE (*Latuca sativa L.*): plant with leaves and oil used in ritual, cosmetic and medical remedies. Narcotic.

LILY (*Lilium Candidum*): flower used in perfume production and medical remedies.

LINSEED (*Linum usitatissimum*): oil-producing seeds of flax plant used in medicine and massage.

LOTUS (*Nymphaea lotus*): used in ritual, the blue lotus (*Nymphaea caerulea*) also used in perfume production and medicine. Aphrodisiac, euphoric.

MARJORAM (*Origanum majorana*): herb used in perfume production, medical and culinary recipes. Anaphrodisiac, antiseptic, digestive, sedative.

MORINGA (*Moringa peregrina*): tree with oil-producing kernels used as base for cosmetics, medicine and massage.

MYRRH (*Commiphora sp*): gum resin used in ritual as incense, in perfume production, cosmetic and medical recipes, massage and mummification. Analgesic, antiseptic, astringent, stimulant.

MYRTLE (*Myrtus communis*): shrub with leaves, flowers and fruit used in cosmetics and perfume production, fumigation and massage. Astringent, antiseptic.

OLIVE (*Olea europaea*): tree with oil-producing fruit used in ritual, perfume production, massage, lighting and cooking.

PEPPERMINT (*Mentha piperata*): herb used in perfume production and medical remedies. Antiseptic, digestive, sedative, stimulant.

PISTACIA (*Pistacia spp.*): gum resin used in ritual and perfume production.

POPPY (*Papaver somniferum*): decorative flower with oil-producing seeds used for medical and culinary purposes. Analgesic, aphrodisiac, euphoric, narcotic, sedative, stimulant.

RADISH (*Raphanus sativus L.*): seed oil used for medicine, massage and culinary purposes.

SAFFLOWER (*Carthamus tinctorius*): plant with decorative flowers and oil-producing seeds used for medical purposes and in dyeing.

SESAME (*Sesamum indicum*): plant with oil-producing seeds used in perfume production, massage, cooking and lighting. Nutritive, emollient.

SWEET FLAG (*Acorus calamus*): plant with root used in perfume production and medicine. Aphrodisiac, sedative.

SYCAMORE FIG (*Ficus sycomorus*): sap, leaves and fruit used in cosmetics, medicine and massage.

THYME (*Thymus spicata*): herb used in perfume production, medicine and cooking. Antiseptic, digestive, expectorant, stimulant.

WORMWOOD (*Artemisia absinthium*): shrub with leaves used in medical remedies and massage. Antiseptic, digestive, stimulant.

BASIC CHRONOLOGY

APPROXIMATE DATES

PREDYNASTIC: PRE-3100 BC

OLD KINGDOM: *C.*3100 BC–*C.*2134 BC

FIRST INTERMEDIATE PERIOD: *C.*2134 BC–2040 BC

MIDDLE KINGDOM: 2040 BC–1640 BC

SECOND INTERMEDIATE PERIOD: 1640 BC–1550 BC

NEW KINGDOM: 1550 BC–1170 BC

THIRD INTERMEDIATE PERIOD: 1170 BC–712 BC

LATE PERIOD: 712 BC–332 BC

GRAECO-ROMAN PERIOD:

PTOLEMAIC PERIOD: 332 BC–30 BC

ROMAN PERIOD: 30 BC–AD 395

BYZANTINE/COPTIC PERIOD: AD 323–642

ARAB CONQUEST: AD 642

AEGEAN

Ilium (Troy)

Boghasköy/Hattusas

ANATOLIA

CASPIAN SEA

Mycenae
Athens
Sparta

CYTHERA

RHODES

Knossos

Phaistos

CRETE

MEDITERRANEAN SEA

Cyrene

Mersa Matruh

Alexandria
Naukratis
Tanis

Siwa Oasis

CYPRUS
(ALASHIYA?)

Ugarit

Enkomi

Byblos
Sidon
Tyre

Megiddo
PALESTINE
Jerusalem
Sharuhen

Carchemish

MITANNI

Ebla

Orontes

SYRIA

Qadesh

Damascus

Jordan

LEBANON

ASSYRIA

Nineveh

Assur

MESOPOTAMIA

Tigris

Euphrates

N

Babylon

BABYLONIA

Susa

PERSIA

Ur

SUMER

Persepolis

Giza
Memphis
Saqqara
Dahshur

Fayum

SINAI

Timna

Serabit el-Khadim
Wadi Maghara

Baharia Oasis

Oxyrhynchus

Amarna

LIBYA

EGYPT

Nile

ARABIA

Farafra Oasis

Abydos

Valley of the Kings
Deir el-Medina
Thebes

Dakhla Oasis

Kharga Oasis

Elephantine

RED
SEA

PERSIAN
GULF

Buhen

Semna

Nile

Kurgus

Gebel Barkal

0   500 km

BIBLIOGRAPHY

CLASSICAL SOURCES

Discorides, trans. J. Goodyer, ed. R. Gunther,
The Greek Herbal of Dioscorides, Oxford 1934
Herodotus, trans. A. de Selincourt, *The Histories*,
Harmondsworth 1954
Homer, trans. E. V. Rieu, *The Odyssey*, Harmondsworth 1946
Pliny the Elder, trans. W. Jones and H. Rackham,
Natural History, Loeb
Theophrastus, trans. A. Hort, *Enquiry into Plants
and Minor Works on Odours and Weather Signs*, Loeb

MODERN SOURCES

Bryan, C. P., *Ancient Egyptian Medicine: The Papyrus Ebers*,
Chicago 1930
— The Chelsea Physic Garden, *Thinking with your Nose:
Plants & the Perfume Industry*, London 1996
Dayagi-Mendels, M., *Perfumes and Cosmetics in the Ancient World*,
Jerusalem 1989
Dixon, D. M., 'The Transplantation of Punt Incense Trees in
Egypt', *Journal of Egyptian Archaeology* 55, 1969, pp.55–65
Fletcher, J., 'Cosmetics and Bodycare', in *Clothing of the Pharaohs*,
ed. G. Vogelsang-Eastwood, Leiden 1994
Fletcher, J., 'Hair Oils', in *Ancient Egyptian Hair: a Study in Style,
Form and Function*, Manchester 1995

Fletcher, J., *Ancient Egyptian Cosmetics & Perfumes*,
London and Austin (in press)
Gore, A., *Reflexology*, London 1990
Hepper, F. N., *Pharaoh's Flowers: the Botanical Treasures
of Tutankhamun*, London 1990
James, T. G. H., *The Mastaba of Khentika called Ikhekhi*, London
1953
Kennet, F., *History of Perfume*, London 1975
Lucas, A., *Ancient Egyptian Materials and Industries*, London 1989
McDermott, S., 'The Soldier's Feet: a short study on medicinal
oils and the military in ancient Egypt', *NILE Offerings* 4,
1998, pp.20-22
Manniche, L., *An Ancient Egyptian Herbal*, London 1989
Nunn, J. F., *Ancient Egyptian Medicine*, London 1996
Rees, A., 'Frankincense and Myrrh', in *Herbs* 20/3, 1995, pp. 9–11
Schoske, S. et al., *Schonheit abglanz der Gottlichkeit*, Munich 1990
Serpico, M. and White, R., 'Oil, Fat and Wax', in *Ancient Egyptian
Materials and Technology*, ed. P. Nicholson and I. Shaw,
Cambridge 1998
Tisserand, R., *The Art of Aromatherapy*, Saffron Walden 1997
Tisserand, R. and Balacs, T., 1995, *Essential Oil Safety:
A Guide for Health Care Professionals*, New York 1995
Van Toller, S. and Dodd, G. H. eds., *Perfumery: The Psychology
& Biology of Fragrance*, London 1988

ILLUSTRATION ACKNOWLEDGEMENTS

Courtesy of the Trustees of the British Museum:
pp. 17, 35 far right, 36 left, 36 below, 37, 40, 57

NILE Archive:
NILE/J. Fletcher: pp. 9, 10, 11 (Cairo Museum),
12, 13, 19, 27, 34 left (Leiden Rijksmuseum),
34 right (Cairo Museum), 35 far left (Metropolitan
Museum of Art, New York), 35 centre (Louvre, Paris),
36 right (Hull Museums), 38 (Metropolitan Museum
of Art, New York), 47 (after James 1953),
51 (Brooklyn Museum), 53
NILE/A. Fildes: pp. 8, 28
NILE/E. Hayes: frontispiece

Hieroglyphs set by Nigel Strudwick using
the Cleo Font designed by Cleo Huggins